THE POWER OF TALKING

THE POWER OF TALKING
Stories from the Therapy Room

Stelios Kiosses

PHOENIX
PUBLISHING HOUSE
firing the mind

First published in 2021 by
Phoenix Publishing House Ltd
62 Bucknell Road
Bicester
Oxfordshire OX26 2DS

British Library Cataloguing in Publication Data

A C.I.P. for this book is available from the British Library

ISBN-13: 978-1-912691-80-7

Typeset by Medlar Publishing Solutions Pvt Ltd, India

www.firingthemind.com

Contents

Preface

I understand that it is difficult for a lot of us to reach out for support and I also understand why psychotherapy can seem extremely uncomfortable for some. I understand these things because I have felt them in my own personal therapy. This book is a reminder that it's OK to be human; it's normal to feel uncomfortable about psychotherapy, and being vulnerable is something most of us don't innately know how to do. What I mean by this is that although vulnerability for many is synonymous with weakness it is an essential element to living wholeheartedly. I believe that in our lives we can't truly form a relationship with at least some degree of vulnerability; we have to open up at some point or another. Being vulnerable and taking steps to trust someone is something that comes with time. Therefore, being vulnerable means to show ourselves to others completely and utterly without holding back for fear of rejection or judgement.

Through the case studies in this book you will encounter various examples of psychological defences. You will come to understand the process of a client in psychotherapy who carries with them a brace of negative symptoms and a spectrum of psychological mechanisms by which he or she keeps a distance from others for fear of getting 'hurt'.

You will come to understand also how a therapist provides a compassionate and corrective experience to their clients by helping them to remove some of these defensive burdens. Through the case studies we will review the theoretical underpinnings and steps that are taken by therapists to reach through to the person beneath these resistances. My therapeutic framework is integrative with a specific emphasis on psychodynamic therapy. Through this mechanism we will look at novel processes such as monitoring unconscious signals and the handling of psychological defences.

The beginning of my personal therapy started when I entered my postgraduate programme in psychodynamic counselling at Oxford University. I remember my course director dropping the bomb that all students were required to undertake personal therapy during the programme in order to graduate. I had not been required to see a therapist in my previous training and I was immediately uncomfortable. Even as a therapist-in-training, I was reluctant to sit down with a total stranger and open up about issues I suspected were there but had no desire to face. I understood later on during my psychodynamic training that resistance is an integral part of this journey. Resistance is what we all do to protect ourselves from an awareness of that which we fear will overwhelm us. It does not happen consciously. Resistance works like friction—in the exact opposite direction that you want to go. And because it is the product of our defences, which are at the core of our personalities, it is very difficult to break through. We resist most the material we most need to address.

When, at the age of seventeen, I declared to my parents, "I want to go and study in [communist] Romania," it was the beginning of my becoming conscious of my decision to study psychology. That and a book called *Breakdown* written by Stuart Sutherland, who later became my supervisor at Sussex University as an undergraduate in experimental psychology. At the time, I saw going to Romania as a challenge and an adventure. My parents finally agreed to let me travel and study there. So after an intense six months of learning Romanian I applied to enter the medical school in Transylvania, the University of Cluj. However, after three years in a communist country with one of the hardest and most corrupt regimes, I decided enough was enough and left for the UK. It was during those years of intense communist unpredictability and working in the most horrifying psychiatric wards that something stirred in me. This stirring happened after witnessing, in these barbaric conditions, human beings silenced and humiliated. I observed personalities being dissolved. It was like working in a slaughterhouse of souls. I witnessed starving and sick children in overcrowded orphanages and experienced first-hand the suffering, desperation, grief and defencelessness displayed in these children's eyes, long before the fall of communism revealed these things to the outside world.

There were two things I remember most vividly, which I initially resisted exploring in my personal therapy but eventually succumbed to during the therapeutic process. They will stay with me forever: I remember a young, eight-year-old girl escaping from a psychiatric ward in the middle of the winter to try to find her parents. She was suffering from depression and had been institutionalised after her parents had abandoned her in the middle of a field at the age of six. There was a desperate need to find her as she could not survive long in the winter conditions and deep snow. I remember the search party coming back empty-handed. They found her one month later, dead, frozen by the bitter winter.

My second memory was that of the silent cries of so many children in an orphanage I had been placed in as part of my medical training. I remember stepping into a room full of cribs, possibly about thirty of them, each containing a child anywhere from a few months to two years old. As I stepped into the room I was deafened by the silence; the room was perfectly peaceful, calm and still. I remember recounting this traumatic memory in a session and my therapist saying, 'Crying is the sound of life.' The child is saying: 'Someone will come. Someone loves me.' None of these children were crying or sleeping. Some sat up in their cribs but most lay on their backs staring into space like vacant corpses. It was a moment that would forever be burned into my heart. These children had been crying out for countless hours and eventually stopped when they realised no one was coming for them. This was quite pertinent in my session as the sense of abandonment was something I experienced from a young age when my father had abandoned me, leaving me with my mother and subsequently with a stepfather.

My personal therapy gave me the platform to discover and explore all these lifetime experiences and make sense of my personal traumas. I came from a very angry household. Dysfunctional, to say the least.

I'd say that I am such a good listener because of the fear that I carried with me for a long time from that abusive childhood. It took me years to come to terms with that in my own personal therapy. Of course, like so many people, I wouldn't trust my therapist to do me any good at first. I had always had to look after myself. But I realised through therapy just how abusive my upbringing had been. I was in therapy for two difficult years, and after that I felt ready to move on with my life.

It is important to remember that people resist without being in therapy. Again, it arises out of our defensive style, our personalities. Like any defence, it protects us from something that hurts. In psychodynamic terms, resistance is the client's attempt to block or repress anxiety-provoking memories and insights from entering conscious awareness.

I had originally trained in a form of therapy named cognitive behavioural therapy. CBT, as it is commonly known, tends to emphasise change via the habit and justification systems, examining actions and beliefs. In contrast psychodynamic therapy tends to emphasise the experiential, relational and defensive systems of adaptation by examining core feelings and subconscious processes. Psychodynamic psychotherapy has its roots in the theories and work of Sigmund Freud and his ideas regarding psychoanalysis. Put simply, psychodynamic psychotherapy stresses the significance of our early childhood experiences and how they continue to affect us during adulthood. In contrast CBT focuses specifically on the problems and difficulties in the present, rather than issues based in the past.

Training initially as an integrative therapist, cognitive behavioural therapist and later as a psychodynamic practitioner at Oxford, was very rewarding. There was a thematic weekend every month covering skills, the body, sexuality, pathology, creative visualisation, childhood and the creative use of pain, crisis and failure. It was about using yourself as a laboratory for growth and development, leading to a deep understanding of what is required for self development and healing. Although a high academic standard was required at Oxford, for me it was the personal commitment and involvement that seemed critical. We could not expect our clients to go anywhere we had not been ourselves. This seems a sound philosophy to me, but I am also aware that it is less of a requirement in many training organisations today or in the previous institutions I trained in.

My childhood experiences of being wounded and my later struggles as an adult have been the primary focus of my own personal therapy. I teach my clients now to forgive themselves (and others), to accept themselves as they are and to embrace their weaknesses as aspects of their uniqueness. However, this valuable wisdom would have not been acquired if I had not undergone therapy myself. I found a counsellor and the experience changed my life, for the better—I learnt how to cope in my life and how to free my real self. I had all the tools within—he taught me that all I needed to do was to find them. And I did. I remain forever grateful for his gentle, patient guidance in that dark, difficult time. I emerged into the sunlight of a new me. Calm and no longer bewildered by life's ups and downs. It was a magnificent and very enduring journey and one I shall never forget.

The transition to train in psychodynamic therapy from CBT came from my own observations when I found that although CBT focused with the clients on strategies that reduced their problematic symptoms, it did not somehow help them gain a deeper insight into their own identity and relationship patterns. Furthermore, it is hard to believe that a simple toolbox of skills is really going to address the fundamental issues of your existence and help you to get to the root of your deep psychological issues which psychodynamic therapy explores. The ability to distract yourself, tolerate pain, calm yourself down, and so forth, seem at best a good set of tools to have when embarking on the emotional work that is the hallmark of psychodynamic therapy. In this book you will find that both therapies are used interchangeably as my approach is that of an integrative therapist, that is, a combined approach to psychotherapy that brings together different elements of specific therapies.

Disclaimer

All of the stories presented in this book, whilst based on real-life cases of mine, are fictitious. To preserve confidentiality and anonymity, all identifying details have been anonymised and pseudonyms are used. The case studies are a composite of clients dealing with similar psychological issues. Any resemblance to persons living or dead is purely coincidental.

ONE

On being a therapist

We therapists are not heroes. We are not special because of the way we listen to troubled people and try to help. We are healers, for the most part. But we are wounded healers. Goethe wrote that our own suffering prepares us to appreciate the suffering of others and it's true that my past wounds have facilitated an empathic connection with my clients. But it was Jung, a Swiss psychiatrist who founded analytical psychology, who first referenced the archetype of the wounded healer, drawing from Greek mythology and exploring applications to psychology.

There was a time when I thought that psychotherapy was something anyone and everyone could do, but now after my own personal therapy I know that not everyone can or should be a therapist. It is not enough, in my opinion, to possess the education and credentials to counsel people; you also need to have the heart, patience and personality. These qualities are as important, if not more so, to undertake this work. Even as a child, I was always a very intuitive and empathic person. I was always in touch with my feelings and would spend hours alone just trying to figure out why I felt a certain way.

There is, however, a risk that therapists are assumed to be 'fixed' after undertaking personal therapy, and once and for all 'relieved from all evil' after such a challenging personal journey. However, this can backfire as not every therapist who has had therapy and can identify with emotional suffering becomes more effective. The characteristic virtue of healing has to be incorporated with other features, like the capacity to control such identifications and be able to process or recycle pleasurable as well as painful life experiences.

What I mean by this is that we can learn from our own experiences and mistakes and also learn from others' experiences and mistakes. We can then reprocess these experiences in a new and different context that is more helpful and adaptive. We reuse the 'waste' and sort it and arrange it in different piles and then we can consider what can be used and where; think of it as emotional recycling. This, I believe, brings up a sense of realisation of multiple truths and perspectives for every situation we encounter within ourselves and others.

Psychotherapy, on the whole, can be very effective. This bears emphasis, because many people are still sceptical that it is an authentic and viable treatment. There is no shortage of empirical evidence demonstrating that psychotherapy helps clients with a wide range of psychological issues, from the relatively simple (fear of flying and spiders) to complex and treatment-resistant conditions such as borderline personality disorder and schizophrenia. It may not help everyone, but neither do a whole host of medicines for physical ailments. The point is, it *does* help a lot of people.

Clients present a large variety of problems when coming for psychotherapy. Problems may vary from the general, such as feeling depressed, to the specific, solving difficulties with a supervisor at work. Often, clients expect that such problems will be resolved, or at least made manageable. In a sense, psychotherapy may be seen as a form of problem-solving. As such, it is an important task to understand how clients describe their difficulties.

You will note that I also use the terms 'counsellor' and 'counselling' in the book. These are often used interchangeably with 'psychotherapist' and 'psychotherapy' and I have followed this convention. There are many similarities between the two disciplines, although psychotherapy usually requires a longer, more in-depth training.

My childhood experiences of being wounded and my later struggles as an adult have been a primary motivator for becoming a therapist—it is often the case. I have learned that although my own wounds may sometimes be activated during a therapy session, they can also potentially be used to promote self-healing within my client. This book is about that healing process. Each case study is not only about the silent voices of my clients' ghosts but the more intimate texture of vulnerability that both client and therapist bring to the arena of therapy.

Feeling properly heard in therapy can be a first-time experience. Families and relationships all have limits, and of course counselling does too, but counsellors allow clients to choose the pace. There is no rush and confidentiality is the touchstone for being able to really trust another person.

Psychotherapy training involves years of personal therapy, and as therapists we are aware of what it's like to sit in the chair, so to speak. It's something clients are usually unaware of, but therapists know how it feels to really open your heart and innermost self—to another human being and know that you are safe with them and that they will be there with you on your journey to becoming whole again.

The way we communicate with clients has also changed in the past twenty years. Technology in a sense has altered the landscape of communication through the use of our personal phones and computers to manage the mental health care of our clients. However, even though all these changes are taking place there is one constant in psychotherapy that remains the same: it is a two-directional 'flow' of therapeutic and emotional influence. What I mean by this is that psychotherapy has an initial 'flow' of impacting our clients' emotional and spiritual state of mind and a 'flow' of affecting us therapists in our personal and professional life by helping us to understand ourselves from those we help.

* * *

So now, almost twenty-five years on, having looked again at my journal from my training years I see that my reasons for wanting to be a psychotherapist remain unchanged. I have changed, as we all do, but the central and most fundamental reason for my beginning my training was because, once, I needed someone to help me through a time in my life that was very, very difficult. For me there is no other profession that can provide you with a complete sense of fulfilment and a continuous growth of learning and challenge. Being a therapist is truly a lifelong journey which we share with others towards healing.

TWO

Gareth

It has taken me years to work out exactly what mood and message I want my consulting room to convey. When clients enter, they are welcomed into a calming space with atmospheric lighting and a large plant—a weeping fig. I have deliberately avoided any resonances with Freud's room, with its dark ambience and a couch covered by a rug. The walls in my room are hung with a significant number of non-representative artworks, which suggest abstract concepts rather than anything tangible, which might be distracting, and my two armchairs have some cushions and a wool blanket for comfort and warmth. There is a full wall of windows with natural light pouring through, and fresh air, when weather permits. It's a place where clients stand on the threshold of something they have been hoping for, perhaps for a long time, where their emotions will finally be understood and their story told. It can be frightening, I know. What if it doesn't work?, is the fear. The carefully designed, controlled space and my presence are there to reassure them. And yet this room has witnessed many of my clients' tears and a few of my own, too.

Therapy, in its best sense, is a process that can be viewed as an inherent and intuitive progression that is often trapped beneath layers of conditioning, fear and reactivity. I have a relationship with my clients that is not romantic, of course, nor is it a friendship, though it is potently full of emotional intimacy and trust. I understand the hope and the trust that they place in me and I can often relate to their pain. There are times when I leave this room and feel deeply satisfied with my day's work. However, there are also times when I can feel tired and burdened by what I've heard, when, as the day goes on, I find I'm increasingly incapable of patience or thoughtfulness. Absorbing another's pain is hard mental labour.

I had experienced one of those days when my less than optimal self was waiting for the last client to arrive. It has been a long day of therapising, all the while being pushed outside my preferred version of myself, the one in which I am truly empathic, as we say in therapy. To achieve this state involves an extreme effort on my part—to listen to the client in such a way that the client feels listened to. Even for a therapist, empathy is sometimes surprisingly difficult to achieve. As human beings, we all have a strong tendency to advise, tell, agree or disagree when someone is telling us their story, and we do this, of course, from our own point of view. As therapists we care for each client, but we don't have a stake in their life. We are neither inclined to tell clients what they want to hear, nor what they don't want to hear. But while I've always considered myself to be a good listener, it is worrying how often I can fail to truly listen to my clients when I am mentally tired.

On this particular evening I was reminded of an exercise I had done as a therapist in training. In one group, each trainee was given an inflated balloon; the other group were given some peas. The second group, in which I was included, were then asked to throw their peas at the balloons. As we watched the peas bouncing off the balloons I finally understood that if we are not receptive to the ideas and the important stories our clients bring to the session then they will bounce off us like peas off a balloon, and we miss the important moments with our clients. Despite my own frustrations that evening it was imperative that I make myself really listen, so I took a moment to prepare myself for what was coming next. Bolstered by coffee, I was hopeful about what could be achieved before I headed home to face my own domestic life.

As the afternoon gave way to early evening, orange rays peeked through the window. The warm glow of the dying sunlight was mesmerising, a real treasure in a normally wintery London. I looked again at my client's referral letter. A colleague, a psychiatrist, had sought my advice regarding what he thought was a sudden turn for the worse in an unmarried man called Gareth, a sixty-year-old retired solicitor. My colleague had been treating Gareth for his depression for almost ten years. Gareth had been hospitalised a number of times during that period and there had been a few serious attempts to take his own life. My colleague had persisted through these crises, making himself emotionally available and medicating Gareth appropriately. He informed me that Gareth rarely said anything about his past, but there was a particular event which had happened during a trip to Germany when he was in his mid-thirties that was clearly central to Gareth's problems.

The story told to me by my colleague was that Gareth had given a ride to a female hitchhiker who had died when his car collided with a truck after its driver had fallen asleep on the motorway. Gareth had always resisted talking about the details of the accident and ever since, for nearly thirty years, had suffered greatly. Now, in the aftermath of Gareth's latest bout of depression and attempted suicide, he had informed my colleague that he finally felt ready to talk to a psychotherapist about his traumatic experience.

Psychotherapists will often work together with psychiatrists for the well-being of our clients, and our jobs very often overlap. But there are several crucial differences between us, the most critical being our approach to treatment. Psychiatrists are trained as medical doctors and can prescribe medications. Thus, they spend much of their time with patients on their medication management. However, psychotherapists focus on assisting our clients to explore and understand aspects of themselves and their experience through talking and applying various psychotherapeutic skills.

People like me help them to understand how past experiences influence and shape their current responses to life events. The focus is on the here and now and the past provides the platform for understanding. On many occasions, clients like Gareth choose to open up and talk to a therapist rather than a psychiatrist because of time constraints. Psychiatric consultations usually last just fifteen minutes. This is largely because there are not enough psychiatrists to meet demand. But psychotherapy is a talking treatment and sessions usually last from fifty to sixty minutes, giving clients ample time to settle in and disclose their innermost feelings.

A recent study suggests that talk therapy may be as good as or even better than drugs in the treatment of depression. I believe medication is important but that it's the relationship that gets people better. Unpacking your emotions takes real effort, and working through them is just that: work. Meeting with a psychiatrist during a 'medication appointment' is usually a very disempowering experience. The client is expected to answer a few perfunctory questions and then they receive their prescription for powerful drugs that can dramatically alter the quality of a life, sometimes for the worse. In these meetings the psychiatrist also assumes a position of power and a client will more often than not fulfil the role of the quiet, unquestioning, passive 'patient'. Psychotherapy couldn't be more different.

One of the most distinctive ways psychiatrists and psychotherapists differ is how we refer to the individuals we see for treatment. This is important as it reflects the words we use on how we think about the help we offer. For example, psychiatrists will refer to the individuals they see as 'patients'. The word patient comes from the Latin 'pati' for 'suffering' meaning 'the one who suffers'. It implies, therefore, a person who receives medical care. 'Patient' also implies a hierarchical relation from doctor to patient. The word 'client', on the other hand, was developed by therapists to signify a rejection of this medical way of treatment, replaced by the notion of psychological growth and healing. We believe that our clients suffer from psychological states of individual and social isolation and as such we guide them to new directions in finding solutions that will empower them and free them from emotional suffering. However, the choice to use the term 'patients' or 'clients' continues to be debated amongst all mental health professionals (psychologists, psychiatrists, social workers, psychotherapists, and so on) and those they are seeking to help.

* * *

At a gentle knock, I opened the door to Gareth. He said a curt hello before I could greet him, and walked into the room ahead of me. There was a soldierly rigidity to his gait that gave me the immediate sense that this wouldn't be easy. But in contrast to his military poise, he looked as though he hadn't shaved in a while. His flushed skin was dashed with grey hairs that weren't long enough or shaped enough to be an intentional beard. He had the look of a man who was once muscular, broad over the back and thick in the neck, but he was carrying some extra weight now that those once honed muscles had turned mostly to fat. He looked very much like any other older man. I wanted to get a sense of him, physically, so I took him in while he was half turned away, busy hanging his coat behind the door.

Gareth spoke in a soft but firm voice that had the huskiness of a smoker. His eyes were pale blue slits, heavily lidded, languorous and indifferent. He had high, arching eyebrows that gave him an inquisitive expression, as though he were always asking a question. And, in this way, I pigeonholed him while, of course, I had no idea what was going on behind the facade.

After sitting in silence for a few minutes I asked him how he was feeling physically. Gareth described the state he was in: 'I feel exhausted and fatigued. No matter how much I sleep, I still feel tired and worn out. Getting out of bed every morning is very hard, even impossible.'

And then I asked: 'How do you feel emotionally?'

He said he has been asked this question many times before but he didn't have any idea what his 'feelings' were. He spoke the word as though it were in inverted commas. He didn't know what the word 'feelings' even meant, he said. He was familiar with his overwhelming depressive state, and he knew about wanting to die. That was all.

Gareth was struggling emotionally in that first session and was unable to be introspective or reflective; he had no vocabulary for expressing what he was experiencing emotionally.

* * *

'How are you feeling?' is a question therapists frequently ask their clients. Unlike the way it can be used as a throwaway nicety in polite society, we are genuinely looking for an answer. But, what is the point of the question? What information are we trying to glean from this seemingly simple enquiry?

There's a long history of people making the connection between the body and the mind and people often mistakenly view depression and other psychological disorders as only emotional. However, mental illness also affects our bodies. Depression is not just an emotion. Its physical effects are real and shouldn't be underestimated. In the *New England Journal of Medicine*, at least 80 per cent of physical symptoms taken to general practitioners are stress related. It should make perfect sense to address the mind's role in our physical ailments and adaptive mental activity in order to reduce the stress and stop our physical symptoms.

Somatic experiencing of psychological manifestations was a concept that was first introduced by Dr Peter Levine in 1997.[1] From his observations of animal behaviour in natural environments, he developed the theory that trauma-related health conditions are psychological manifestations of physiological phenomena. So, for example, if we are threatened, we go into fight, flight or freeze mode. Our survival brains take over, and we experience an enormous surge of energy as our bodies flood with the body chemicals needed to escape or flee.

Most of our clients will not have experienced any real threat, so this 'energy' stays in the nervous system and is expressed through physical movements like shaking, yawning, tingling or crying. In nature, the healthy release of traumatic energy can be seen in animals that shake after escaping a predator. For us humans this 'cut off' release is experienced with physical symptoms such as digestive problems and sleep disturbances, along with serious, persistent emotional distress.

Over the years I have observed that the majority of my clients are inclined to disrupt this process of the physical signs of release. The body is elegantly designed to heal. The body really wants to heal. It really wants to be regulated. But when clients tell themselves 'not to cry', 'not to shake', etc., because they 'feel' uncomfortable expressing this emotion, the natural healing process of our genetic make-up is interfered with. In therapy, we encourage our clients to trust their body and not to override it with negative beliefs and negative thoughts and behaviours.

One way I help clients to achieve this is through a strategy called resourcing. This process works by empowering the conscious mind to cope with the overwhelming nervous responses. It involves thinking of a place or a memory that brings calm, peacefulness or happiness and allows you to experience the physical release of energy without

---

[1] Levine, P. A. (1997). *Waking the Tiger: Healing Trauma—The Innate Capacity to Transform Overwhelming Experiences*. Berkeley, CA: North Atlantic.

producing heightened emotional distress. A resource is anything that you notice helps you to bring your body down from a state of hyper-arousal. It is also referred to as a window of tolerance describing the zone of arousal in which a person is able to function most effectively.

If there's something you hate to do, like visiting the dentist or flying, think about a so-called 'happy place' which you go to that helps you get through it, if you can put yourself there, in your mind. This is an extremely useful tool for clients who want to continue using an effective coping strategy that they can carry with them far beyond their time in therapy. I believe that conscious exploration and integration of the mind–body interface and the establishment of a mindful presence is the cornerstone of transforming much of the disconnection and suffer-ing we see in our clients.

* * *

Gareth and I spent our first few sessions in silence. Silence is often seen as an accepted and even expected part of the conversation in therapy, although in normal interaction a lot of people panic if silence falls! Silence can be an important tool that allows the therapist to better understand the therapeutic relationship, the client's conflicts and defences, resis-tances, adaptive functioning and interpersonal style. I wasn't concerned by the silence with Gareth; you can learn a great deal from silence. My role lies somewhere between being the silent, absorbed and active listener, and the motivational drill sergeant.

Gareth arrived again the following week for his session. After a while, again sitting in silence with him, he suddenly decided to speak about his experience in Germany, briefly explaining what happened.

With a trembling voice he told me: 'All I want to say at this moment is that it is my fault.'

I asked him what he meant by that.

He explained: 'It is my fault that she died. I should be the one who's dead, not her.'

Gareth then stopped and retreated back into his silent mode.

Immediately after his remark I had a very strange experience. I was looking at the wall behind Gareth and the shadow of a girl seemed to appear, in the way that light causes shadows and from them the mind creates shapes we understand. It was an extraordinary feeling. I thought I was imagining things. But the form was so clear, I wondered if this was something significant for me to pay attention to. Although Gareth hadn't yet spoken in detail about the accident in Germany and the girl's death he had expressed enough for me to be able to 'project' about her.

* * *

Projections often happen at times of crisis and stress, when feelings become unmanageable. Rather than admitting, accepting and owning your own thoughts, feelings and behaviours, it's easier to put them onto someone else. Projection is an unconscious process that happens automatically and is not usually planned or well thought out. Freud first used the concept of projection to explain and address the process of externalising an individual's feelings. He further defined the concept as a defence mechanism against the internal anxiety that the individual couldn't otherwise deal with. Freud believed that an individual uses it to help protect himself from a perceived threat. He thought an individual might also use it to reduce anxiety and avoid any conflict, if at all possible.

Later on that day, in supervision, I talked about what had happened. Supervision is the formal, contractual arrangement between a therapist and an experienced, appropriately qualified colleague in which we agree to meet on a regular basis to reflect on and discuss our clinical work. In supervision, the therapist can talk about any challenges they've faced in their client work, any concerns they have about the way they're working with a client, and any feelings of doubt.

It's vital in therapeutic work that we absorb and understand the projected feelings of our clients and use this information to try to understand what is going on for the client. However, not even in supervision could we make sense of the shadow I'd seen. And it wouldn't make any real sense until after Gareth fully revealed his story, a secret he had lived with for a long time. But that was some time away. Until then I could only rationalise that my seeing the shadow of a girl was something to do with what I was not able to hear from Gareth or feel from our limited conversation. In hindsight, it's as though Gareth was telling me something, his unconscious communicating with my unconscious.

In the meantime, we were still sitting in silence each session and I was waiting patiently and supportively for Gareth to start to talk. But I knew I wasn't paying enough attention to the experience of simply sitting with him. When I lecture I always tell my students: 'Listen very closely to your client's words. Much of what you'll need to help your client with therapy you'll hear in the first two minutes of the session, and there's usually a metaphor in there somewhere.'

Gareth's statement—'I don't even know what feelings mean'—was my prompt to ask him to express what it means not to 'understand' his feelings.

He responded by saying, 'It's like a shadow above my head.'

And perhaps that was exactly what I saw, I just didn't understand at the time. The metaphor described his experience.

* * *

In the next few sessions we spent the majority of the time in silence again but I did attempt to unpack his metaphor a little further when he came for his tenth session. I asked him about the shape, the size, the movements of his shadow. He described the shadow as being that of a young girl hovering above his head—the girl I'd 'seen'.

I pushed him further: 'How do you feel about seeing this shadow?'

The process of psychotherapy can be frightening for clients like Gareth, especially when we don't really understand what it's 'supposed' to look like or why sitting in a room with another person somehow helps us make lasting changes to our lives. Using metaphors like a 'shadow' as part of the psychotherapy process is not uncommon. As therapists we often use metaphors with our clients to foster increased understanding of an experience or a series of experiences. Shared understanding of experiences allows us to communicate using the same language and, ultimately, to better explore the changes we seek to make.

Research has shown that metaphor usage is connected to emotional change and, specifically, there is support for an increased occurrence of metaphors when talking about emotions, especially intense emotions. It allows us to step outside the emotion, to view it more objectively. Metaphors can also provide a picture which helps others enter your world. It's true that a picture is often worth a thousand words, but a word picture (a metaphor) can sometimes do the same. Climbing a mountain is a great metaphor for many challenges in our lives.

Gareth took a few minutes to respond. Eventually, he hesitantly told me that he was feeling quite fearful about telling me what was going on in his head. He admitted to being torn between protecting himself and allowing me to help him. He took a long pause and added: 'I know I can talk to you, but I have all these fears. I'm worried about what you will think if I tell you what is going on in my mind.' And isn't the thought that what is going on in our heads might completely horrify another person what often holds us back? That, I would suggest, is what therapy is for. It's a place where nothing we think or divulge will have the therapist running for the hills!

I reassured Gareth that, as his therapist, he could trust me and could disclose whatever he felt comfortable with, in his own time. An intuitive therapist knows that everything that happens in the client–therapist relationship is grist for the mill, from the first phone call to the last session. All experiences can be processed into something productive. The destructive can be remade into the generative. As a therapist, my job is to provide the safest healing space, free from my own needs and ego. Knowing that and standing by it deepens the work, the mutual respect with the client and the potential for the best and deepest healing to take place.

As the sessions progressed and Gareth finally began to talk, something in me decided not to ask him about the silent sessions. I guessed he had a need for autonomy and control that was not being lived out in other areas in his life. So, he lived it out with me here in the room, in the silence. It was his therapy, after all, not mine. Client autonomy is one of the five principles the therapeutic boundaries are based upon and are best described by the following:

1. Beneficence: a counsellor must accept responsibility for promoting what is good for the client with the expectation that the client will benefit from the counselling sessions.
2. Nonmaleficence: the idea of doing no harm. The counsellor must avoid at all times (even inadvertently) any activities or situations with the client that could cause a conflict of interest.
3. Autonomy: the counsellor's ethical responsibility to encourage client independent thinking and decision-making, and to deter all forms of client dependency.

4. Justice: the counsellor's commitment to provide an equal and fair service to all clients regardless of age, gender, race, ethnicity, culture, disability and socio-economic status.
5. Fidelity: being honest with clients and faithfully honouring the counsellor's commitment to the client's progress.[2]

We continued with weekly sessions and at some point down the road I checked in with Gareth as to whether the sessions were helpful to him. He assured me that they were but that, for the most part, he just wanted to sit quietly and think.

On this tenth visit, however, he finally decided to disclose his story, the tragic secret that had haunted him for almost thirty years. This thing that had happened when he was in his forties had defined his entire life. He had been receiving help with it for many years and yet could not get any closer to resolution. Telling me what had happened all those years ago when he was still a young man was a huge deal.

Slowly, the story emerged.

Gareth used to be a successful European lawyer and, because his law firm was based both in the UK and Germany, he would travel by car from London to Munich several times a year. He was returning in his car from Germany when he stopped to offer a young woman in her early twenties, who had been hitchhiking through Europe, a lift to London. He explained that her name was Daphne and that she was originally from London—she had seen from his number plate that he was from the UK and might be able to help her with her journey. She was a philosophy student taking a year out to travel Europe and it was time to return home.

Gareth and Daphne spent two days travelling by car, talking non-stop, and fell in love along the way. Gareth was conscious of the age gap but simply could not resist this young woman. The attraction he felt for her was extremely powerful.

'We had so much in common,' he quietly told me. 'We connected immediately. It seemed that everything she loved, I loved. I noticed that we even had the same posture, the same way of carrying ourselves in the world.'

---

[2] Herlihy, B., & Corey, G. (1996). *Boundary Issues in Counseling: Multiple Roles and Responsibilities*. 3rd edition. Alexandria, VA: American Counseling Association, 2015.

But while still in Germany they were involved in a serious accident. Mid-conversation, Gareth was blindsided by a lorry entering an intersection and going way too fast.

'This is an incredibly hard thing for me to talk about,' Gareth said. 'And it shouldn't really be about me. It should first and foremost be about the girl I killed—about Daphne and the family and friends she left behind to grieve, and the devastation it caused them.'

I acknowledged the truth of that but encouraged Gareth to try to express what had happened just after the accident, telling him that it would be good for him to talk it through. He told me that the events were a bit of a blur, but that he remembered an ambulance arriving quickly, as did the police. He was taken to the local police station to give a statement. He tried several times to ask about Daphne; he was worried for her but nonetheless assumed that she would survive. After all, he hadn't sustained any serious injuries. Eventually, he was led out of the interview room to be told by a group of assembled police that Daphne had died on the way to hospital. The news that she hadn't survived knocked him off his feet, and he fell into a chair, where the police left him alone to process the catastrophe.

He remembers going through her belongings, having grabbed her bag when the ambulance arrived, trying to find a contact telephone number for her parents. He eventually found her home number and made the hardest call of his life.

While talking hesitantly to Daphne's mother, he discovered, to his immense shock, that she was his ex-partner—a woman called Maria who had been in his life over twenty years ago. Imagine that! It is almost inconceivable to comprehend how this information would have impacted on Gareth. He had abandoned Maria while she was pregnant with his child; he had been young and fearful of committing himself to a relationship. He had never made any effort. Even with all my years of experience, it would be impossible to grasp the myriad of emotions unleashed at a time when Gareth was already so vulnerable.

* * *

This epiphanic experience has been variously defined by many as 'chance', something out of the ordinary, a random conjoining of inexplicable events that defies our sense of the reasonable. What happens in most of our lives is beyond our control. No matter how carefully you design your life, you cannot know how that design will be affected by a single random event. One small detail can and will change everything. The most carefully planned project can be ruined or created by a single chance event. We call this synchronicity. When you are in sync with the 'thing' that you want you are much more likely to meet that 'thing'. That is why similar people always seem to meet; they are tuned to the same frequency. Synchronicity is an unconscious awareness of life. My own ability to observe, track, integrate and interpret synchronicity patterns in therapy has evolved substantially over the years. I am sceptical and being appropriately sceptical is a vital part of the therapeutic process, but that does not grant me a licence to refuse to believe my client simply because it makes me feel psychologically or emotionally uncomfortable.

* * *

In his book *Coincidences: Chance or Fate* Ken Anderson[3] spent years documenting a series of coincidences drawn from real life. Among the many coincidences that Anderson introduces in his book is an event that took place during the summer of 1979 in Norway, published from the local daily paper. Robert Johansen, fifteen years old, was fishing in a fjord when he caught a beautiful cod of ten pounds that he proudly carried to his grandmother, Thekla Aanen, for lunch. One can imagine the astonishment of the woman when, cleaning up the fish, she found in the stomach the diamond ring heirloom that the women in the family had handed down from generation to generation that had been lost many years ago and had finally returned home.

Unfortunately, there is no scientific or objective way to determine whether synchronicity is valid or not. There is, however, recent research that tries to explain scientifically how we can identify, understand, and perhaps even control the frequency of coincidences in our everyday lives. Dr Bernard Beitman, a leading expert on coincidence studies, proposes[4] the notion of 'grid cells' located in the brain, near the

---

[3] Anderson, K. (1995). *Coincidences: Chance or Fate*. New York: Blandford.
[4] Beitman, B. D. (2016). *Connecting with Coincidence: The New Science for Using Synchronicity and Serendipity in Your Life*. Deerfield Beach, FL: Health Communications.

hippocampus, as an attribution to synchronicity. Dr Beitman explores theories from quantum physics to human psychology to explain synchronistic events usually attributed to luck, paranormal happenings or religion. Beitman provides personal experiences, historical events, and other stories to document events that defy the odds of probability and change lives. Even more interestingly, he looks at the roles that individuals play in creating and observing coincidences, especially during times of intense emotion, need and transition.

Synchronicity and chance can also operate in reverse, and meaningful coincidences can be unpleasant. If you say, 'I'm going to be late' or 'I'm unlucky', then the law of synchronicity works against you. The psychologist Carl Jung initially used the term synchronicity in his 1952 essay, 'Synchronicity: An Acausal Connecting Principle',[5] to describe chance happenings between unconnected people or events. Another term Jung used was the 'collective unconscious'. We are all connected by our unconscious minds. Consciousness and matter are linked. We might look different, but we are all made of the same stuff. A mountain, a tree, a person: we are all made of the same ingredients.

Whether you refer to twists of fate or coincidences these are remarkable occurrences, just like Gareth's, that need analysing and reflecting upon in therapy. Nevertheless, synchronicity is an interesting philosophical idea and at the end of the day what matters in our relationships with each other is trust. Trust is a major ingredient (and arguably even the most important one) in determining if our relationships will work or not. Trust is a massive concept, with definitions that change depending on the discipline it is being defined within. I believe that trust is a human impulse for survival, as well as the driving force that keeps us moving forward in life.

* * *

In our next session I asked Gareth how he felt. He told me that he felt nothing now, just a detachment from reality and from people. But he was clear that having to leave the police station to go back to a hotel room in

---

[5] Jung, C. G. (1952). *Synchronicity: An Acausal Connecting Principle*. Princeton, NJ: Princeton University Press, 1960.

order to phone Daphne's parents in the UK at three in the morning, to tell them that their daughter had been killed in a road traffic accident, while he was at the wheel, was the hardest thing he had ever had to do. He had no way of knowing how Daphne's parents might react. But however he had imagined that difficult conversation going, it could not have been anything like the one he ended up having.

'I was stunned by her mother's response,' Gareth told me. 'I can't remember her exact words but I recall the sentiment vividly. After telling her who I was, in her shock and surprise, and through her tears, she said: "Gareth, it's me, Maria! We were together for a year and you left me when I was pregnant with Daphne. She is your daughter."'

He also remembered clearly the feeling he had when he woke up the next morning in his hotel room. For a split second it was a normal day. He was a successful solicitor returning to the UK from business abroad, and the world was an exciting place. But the events of the night came flooding back to him. A darkness descended and he was overtaken by a belief that he did not have the right to go on living.

'I had taken another person's life. My daughter's life. And I had also had sex with her. I felt like killing myself.'

We had to stop the session at that point. Gareth was completely overwhelmed by his disclosure and was feeling too numb to talk any further.

When faced with extreme situations such as childhood abuse, trauma or grief, it is natural for the body and mind to go into a numbing mode. It's part of what we call the 'freezing response'. As mentioned earlier, as mammals we are wired for fight or flight, an automatic biochemical reaction in both humans and animals that enables us to rapidly produce sufficient energy to flee or fight in a threatening situation. This automatic reaction propels us into action during times of danger. However, few people are aware that the freeze response, also mentioned earlier, is an equally important and related survival mechanism. The phrases 'scared stiff' or 'frozen with fear' reflect this mammalian characteristic. A deer that's 'frozen in the headlights' is responding likewise. However, sometimes such a protective reflex remains in place for a long time after the actual trauma has passed and becomes a way of life. This is how a client like Gareth becomes emotionally detached, and experiences life in a 'dissociated' or 'depersonalised' way. Gareth had been feeling frozen like this for thirty years.

In his next session, Gareth wanted to express the closeness he had felt towards Daphne. At the start of our session I asked him how he had become physically close to her.

He told me that when they met for the first time there was an instant attraction. They decided after a few hours to take a break from driving and have a pit stop. They pulled in to a parking lot for a rest and he remembers how they kept looking into one another's eyes, until eventually she reached out and touched his cheek with her hand.

'I could feel her soft skin touch my cheek,' Gareth told me. He held her hand and waited for a few moments before they moved into an embrace.

I asked Gareth what he loved about Daphne at that moment.

'She was effortlessly beautiful!' he exclaimed. 'I remember how her deep brown eyes took over my soul and wrapped themselves around my heart. She had a sculpted figure, which was slender and lithe, her waist was tapered and she had a fair complexion. I remember she had a bouncy personality and a sugary voice, which I loved. I remember while sitting next to each other in the car that she came up close to me with a look that said "Don't move, trust me", and so I stayed still. She closed her eyes and kissed me deeply.'

Gareth and Daphne had sex in the car, sex which Gareth describes as the most intense sex he'd ever engaged in. 'The kissing was the most extreme and soulful I've ever experienced. But she was my daughter! And I didn't know! I feel so ashamed. I just want to end this pain and suffering. She isn't even alive for me to say I am sorry, darling, for what I have done to you. Please, please forgive me!'

I sympathised with Gareth that having to hide the full nature of his relationship with Daphne from the world must have been difficult for all these years.

'Not one person in my life knows the full, true nature of what happened. You are the first person to know,' he told me.

* * *

The most fruitful approach in therapy is the one that encourages the client to be him- or herself. If you ask anyone what most likely makes a person feel safe, secure and comfortable the answer is an environment of acceptance. Humans are relationship-seeking creatures. As humans, we need to feel that we belong, to feel accepted by others. Encouraging clients to be themselves is allowing them to accept their painful emotions. It's very hard to deal with emotions that are extreme and sometimes even scary; however, accepting your emotions can help to improve your emotion regulation and lead to fewer mood swings and more emotional balance. Emotions are part of a complex system that helps us decide what we should stay away from and what we should approach. Emotions also help us keep lasting relationships with other people. Without emotions, we would make terrible decisions all the time. Accepting emotions is helpful, because when we listen to our emotions, we can actually learn important information.

Carl Rogers,[6] one of the most influential psychological thinkers of the twentieth century, argued that to facilitate genuine psychological and emotional healing, therapists must establish a particular kind of empathic relationship with their clients, one based on the therapist's unconditional acceptance of the client, regardless of what the client says or does or feels. This unconditional acceptance is vital to therapeutic success. In order to unearth the real self the therapist must help the client to feel completely safe from evaluation, judgement or critical scrutiny. Only by providing a safe and accepting environment within which the client can freely explore and learn to accept his or her real self can the therapist facilitate genuine and lasting therapeutic change and real healing.

Being unconditionally accepting of my client allows them to feel safe enough to finally disclose their innermost pain. I can ask the questions that need to be asked, and hope to get an honest and helpful answer.

* * *

I asked Gareth what his love life had been like before meeting Daphne, and he told me that before Daphne, he didn't know what was missing, only that he didn't quite feel like he belonged with anybody. I think a lot of people can relate to that feeling. We go through the motions and to all intents and purposes it looks like we are doing fine. Only we know that something is missing and often even we cannot say precisely say what that is.

---

[6] Rogers, C. R. (1961). *On Becoming a Person: A Therapist's View of Psychotherapy.* London: Constable & Robinson, 2004.

'When she came into my life, it was like the whole world had stopped and for once everything was perfect. I was home, my heart was at ease and I finally knew what love was in its most amazing form,' Gareth explained. 'But I can see now this was the love I had as a parent towards their child!'

* * *

From Gareth's description of the relationship it was obvious that both his and Daphne's unconscious minds wanted to have the intimate closeness, touch and feel of father and child. That force of nature can be so powerful that, in their ignorance, without being aware of the constraints of societal norms, they allowed their emotions to run freely. Sexual attraction between parents or siblings who meet later in life is a recognised phenomenon that, although rare, can happen. We are drawn to what is familiar.

However, the concept of normalising incest, even in a case of 'consensual' genetic sexual attraction (GSA), is extremely complicated, especially when it involves an older parent and a younger person who may be too immature to understand. GSA is a disorder where a person develops strong feelings of sexual attraction towards a family member, whether a cousin, a sibling or half sibling, parent or grandparent. Mating with a relative because there is no one else around has been part of human history for thousands of years. In Gareth's case, the key point is that he was not aware that Daphne was his daughter. So the crucial question is whether it was incest or just a sexual encounter? And why couldn't Gareth forgive himself when the mistake he made was genuine? Perhaps more importantly, why did he feel that society couldn't forgive him? These sorts of taboos are ingrained in us. Imagine yourself in Gareth's position. What would you feel? Everything we have been told and learned has made us react with horror at the very suggestion of a parent having sex with their child.

It was a complex case and one that my academic training could never have prepared me for. Many of my clients who have experienced trauma of the same intensity as Gareth's have had difficulties forming healthy attachments. Earning the trust of a patient like Gareth as a therapist is incredibly difficult as the fear of abandonment can be crippling for this client group.

* * *

I continued seeing Gareth on a weekly basis. In one of our sessions he asked me what I thought about his condition or, more specifically, what did I think he was suffering from? I explained to him that in my opinion he was suffering from complex grief combined with depression and trauma. I told him that grief is an inevitable part of life and that, usually, grief resolves itself. It may never entirely fade, but it almost always changes and becomes incorporated into daily life, so the grieving person can move on.

However, when grief doesn't take this relatively straightforward path towards resolution we call it 'complicated grief' or 'complex grief'. This type of grief results from challenging and often ambivalent relationships, leaving the survivor with unresolved feelings of guilt, shame, anger and regret that can fester, sometimes for many years. As therapists, negotiating the troubled waters of complex grief can be difficult. In effect, because one person in a complicated relationship has died we're challenged to find a solution to an equation with only half the factors at our disposal. Gareth and Daphne comprised such a difficult 'equation'.

Because of all the traumatic events surrounding Gareth's experience he had several layers of psychological trauma that had to be worked through. In an effort to prevent destabilising any emotional well-being he had been able to take from our sessions over the last six months, it was important to work with one issue at a time. Daphne's death and his chronic grieving seemed like a natural place to start, as Gareth had been mourning the loss of his daughter for the last thirty years.

The social stigma and shame associated with GSA meant that Gareth had denied himself the ability to grieve for his child and deal with the guilt associated with her loss and subsequent feelings. When Daphne died, Gareth was grief-stricken, but even thirty years after her death, many of Gareth's symptoms remained unchanged: daily tearfulness, extreme anxiety, helplessness, deeply entrenched feelings of guilt and social isolation. These problems seemed to go beyond simple mourning. For Gareth, these suppressed feelings had become self-destructive and were being projected outwardly in the form of rage or inwardly in the form of self-hatred. Validating Gareth's grief and allowing him a safe place to openly mourn his loss became our primary therapeutic goal.

* * *

In the eighth month of therapy, during a Friday night session in June, Gareth and I sat together through an unexpected London thunderstorm. For nearly an hour, the city experienced a riveting weather event. I remember seeing a brilliant blue flash of lightning flame, followed by the noise of a loud thunderclap.

During this session Gareth felt uneasy and unsafe. He said that these weather conditions reminded him of Daphne, because the evening of the accident had been a thundery night. The loud noises caused Gareth's angry, violent feelings to build and reverberate within him. He explained that immediately after the accident and throughout his psychiatric treatment across all these years, he had continued to have frightening nightmares of bloody mayhem all around him, as well as a repetitive dream in which he found himself running towards the car to save Daphne. He would then wake up frightened, crying, and unable to go back to sleep.

I asked him why he thought he was having the same dream over and over again. Having recurring dreams is a common phenomenon, with two thirds of us experiencing them. These dreams may not always mean that you are obsessed with something or someone, but may symbolise your feelings and worries. It is unlikely that the dreams are exactly the same each time, but the recurring theme is usually something in your head that is somehow unresolved. I asked Gareth if he thought that was a reasonable summary of what was happening to him, and he agreed that it was. Once the conflict in his mind was resolved, through therapy, the recurring dreams should end.

Gareth's symptoms and repetitive dreams are a symbolic expression of internal conflict and fear. Fearful of the eruption of dangerous impulses, he had learned to shut down, and yet these feelings were still able to seep out. The internal threat preoccupied his mind, so that he could not concentrate, enjoy himself, or sleep. If he allowed the 'letting go' that sleep involves, his violent feelings might get out of control, as indeed they were doing, in his dreams.

It was time to explore the work needed for him to come to terms with his grief. I asked him how he felt about the fact that Daphne was no longer here.

'I feel lost,' he told me. 'Like I don't really know how to do things or live my life.'

'Can you tell me how you felt just after she died, at the time?'

'I was really scared, guilty and angry,' Gareth responded. 'I didn't know how I would be able to cope.'

Was he telling me that he felt the same now as he did thirty years ago?

'I guess I do,' he confirmed. 'What's wrong with that?'

Grief is a process which has a number of stages, I explained: denial, anger, bargaining, depression, acceptance. However, we also know that the grieving process is complex, isolating and ongoing—requiring emotional energy to find meaning in the vast unfairness. This goes on under the skin, invisible to the outside world.

I explained to Gareth that in order for him to deal with his grief he needed to be able to move through all the stages until he came to a level of acceptance and optimism about the future. We may not move through the various stages in a straight line, often we go forwards and then backwards again, in a regressive move, and this might happen several times, but we do need to keep on trying to move forward. The way grief is experienced and expressed is unique to each of us and shaped by the nature of the relationship we had with the person who has died, the circumstances of their death, our past experience of loss as well as the culture in which we live. The process of adapting to a significant loss can vary dramatically from one person to another. It often depends on a person's background, beliefs, and relationship to what was lost.

The first stage of grief is accepting that your loss has really happened, experiencing the pain that comes with grief, trying to adjust to life without the person who died, and putting less emotional energy into your grief and finding a new place to put it so that you can move on. But although Gareth was intellectually able to understand the grieving process, and the series of emotions he should have felt over the years, he still felt unable to deal with his daughter's death. Sometimes people grieve for years without seeming to find even temporary relief. Sometimes, I told him, there is an issue associated with the loss, which prevents us from grieving effectively. This may be some sort of unfinished business with the person who has died or a belief that someone won't cope without the lost person.

Grief can be complicated by other conditions, most notably depression. The person's level of dependency on the departed can also cause complications. It may be that other, subsequent losses, which haven't been fully addressed, become caught up with this unresolved loss, making it seem as fresh as ever, even decades later. Or sometimes we look for forgiveness but we feel too depressed and angry to ask for it. This resistance to forgiveness due to anger is not uncommon in therapy. Even if anger, guilt or fear is acknowledged as a problem, the patient feels helpless or unable to actually let go of the emotion.

'But *how* do I let it go?' is one of the questions I hear most often in my consulting room. This is a positive moment because the person is now aware of the problem and is looking for a way to fix it. It is an excellent introduction to understanding the psychological process that keeps us inert. The process focuses on letting go of guilt, anger and fear. These emotions are the 'glue' that holds negative beliefs in place, ensuring that the cognitive-emotional patterns that block happiness and peace remain. I see therapy as a cognitive-emotional process, with forgiveness as a central issue and technique. No matter what the level of developmental arrest, as soon as forgiveness is embraced, negative beliefs can be replaced by positive ones. This, quite simply, leads to a better life.

I asked Gareth what he thought the issue was that had prevented him from moving on with Daphne's death.

Gareth replied: 'I guess, for me, it is asking for forgiveness from her.' I told him, 'Forgiveness is about accepting for yourself that the event has been resolved and that you need no longer carry that burden around with you. It's a critical piece of the grieving process: letting go of what's gone before so that you can move forward with your own life.'

Gareth wanted to know how he should go about forgiving himself.

I told him that a good start would be writing a letter to Daphne about their relationship and his feelings. This would be a safe expression of his raw grief. As the grieving process is not linear, within that process there is a huge range of emotions: shock, disbelief, confusion, sadness, guilt, anger, fatigue—to name just a few. We can become physically ill if we do not give voice to these powerful emotions. Letter writing can often activate strong feelings of grief and sadness and people may well cry as they do it. For some this is very helpful because they are then better able to work on their pain (rather than avoiding it, getting angry with it or trying to bully themselves out of it) and this can be followed by feelings of peace.

'Don't censor your writing,' I told Gareth. 'Use powerful language and say everything you need to say to her. But most importantly you can bring the letter to your next session to read it out loud for us to explore.'

* * *

These letters are not intended to be sent to the person they are addressed to, should they still be alive, but are there to help process strong emotions like anger and depression that reside in a client's mind. Therapeutic letters are intended to develop the work of therapy beyond the consulting room by extending the meaning-making that has already begun in the therapeutic process. The letters help clients identify and channel difficult feelings in a way that maybe they can not in a therapy session. In this way the clients finally get release and freedom from them by expressing these difficult feelings through a safe medium. The letter-writing process is inherently collaborative and enables the client to work at his or her own pace while also facilitating client empowerment and healing.

* * *

I knew the process would help Gareth by giving voice to the unspoken things he wanted to say to his daughter. As he wrote, he had the sensation that he was telling her how he felt. He brought the letter to our next session and through it began not only to convey his feelings for her but to ask for forgiveness. This took several sessions to explore fully. However, one session was particularly poignant.

Gareth told me that the writing exercise had helped him release feelings he felt had been locked inside, feelings that had previously felt 'trapped'. It's the simple process of getting something 'off our chest'. It can be cathartic.

Gareth's feelings had moved from being internally constrained to externally expressed, even if Daphne wasn't physically present to receive the emotional outpouring. The exercise helped him to reaffirm his love for his daughter and begin to forgive himself for unknowingly having had sex with her. When he read the letter out loud, Gareth's face was drawn and clouded; he sat crumpled in his chair, arms crossed tightly around himself, as if the weight of his loss made it impossible to sit up straight. It felt to him as though Daphne had died just the day before. Here is an extract:

> I'm not looking for understanding or forgiveness, I truly feel remorseful for the things that I did. Not only am I remorseful for the abandonment that occurred, now I realise the emotional and

sexual encounter was unspeakable when we met in Germany. I know you did not have the chance of finding out I was your father and you passed away not knowing this. I'm not sure if I can ever make up for what I did to you but believe me, it haunts me every day. I am not perfect nor do I pretend to be, but what I do know is, if I had the chance to do everything over again, I would have hugged you instead of hurting you.

If I could relive those moments back in Germany and if I knew you were my child, I would have just walked away and never touched you. My inappropriate actions have caused me tremendous pain and suffering, and I take full responsibility, I hold myself 100% accountable. And this is something I'm not proud of. I'm truly ashamed of my actions. When I saw you I saw a light so bright that I couldn't ignore. You, in all your brilliance, made me want to be as close to you as possible. I wanted to know you. I wanted to be with you. From the moment I heard your voice I knew that you were a special person. We talked for hours in the car and shared our most intimate secrets. We laughed, played, and laughed some more in the short amount of time we met. I wanted all of these things and I had no clue that you were my child.

Sometimes I feel evil knowing that I did what I did to you. Sometimes I feel like hell would be too good for me, but then again I wish for hell because the pain of the fire would be a constant reminder of the pain I live with every day knowing what I have done. I am so sorry and I wish I could turn back the clock but I can't. In my heart, I tell myself I love you as my child. My words beg your forgiveness. I love you and I miss you. I'm so very sorry I never got to hold you in my arms or gaze into your eyes or stroke your hair or kiss your cheeks. I love you, Daphne, and I wish the circumstances were different. I promise I will see you again, and next time, you can call me Daddy.

* * *

Gareth continues to undergo psychotherapeutic treatment and Daphne's loss in time has become a more tolerable process. Gareth continues to be motivated and we have reached the goal of diminishing his depression and dealing with his grief over Daphne. He has more energy, will-power, interests. There is less self-criticism. His suicidal thoughts have disappeared.

Gareth's complicated grief is more chronic and more emotionally intense than more typical grief, and it stays at acute levels for much longer. Such grief often follows particularly difficult losses that test a person's emotional and social resources, and where the mourner was deeply attached to the person they are grieving. The passage of time often seems the only remedy for grief, but time didn't help Gareth. In the years following Daphne's tragic death, he felt consumed by grief.

Of course, there's nothing we can do to fill the absence of loved ones and ultimately we must accept the fact that they're not here any more. But acceptance doesn't change the likelihood that many of us will feel emotions like bitterness, anger, longing and loneliness every time we think about them and wish they were still here with us.

THREE

Helen

On one particular morning my first client was running a few minutes late. Helen had phoned reception to say she was stuck in traffic. Timekeeping habits are not irrelevant. Some clients make a point of showing up precisely on time for their session, and this is a conscious decision to avoid having to sit in the waiting room for any period of time. Others arrive late, which also delivers a message that, clearly, they'd rather not do this at all. The therapeutic encounter starts when a client looks at the therapist's website, continues when the appointment is made by phone or email, but it's in the waiting room that it solidifies. There, things become real.

Psychotherapy can take place in a range of settings, of course: hospitals, schools, universities or perhaps the therapist's own home. If clients arrive in an agitated state they won't necessarily notice the décor of the therapist's consulting room or the finer details of the practice waiting room. Their focus is solely on the chance to speak to their therapist. Nonetheless, the overall mood of the environment may be significant in helping clients feel more at ease and there is now research suggesting that the counselling environment has the potential to affect a client's sense of psychological and physiological well-being. This applies not just to the therapist's room but to the waiting room, too. It's a holistic experience.

As psychotherapy can be a complicated process for a client, they resort to evaluating the therapeutic experience based on what they can understand of it. That understanding, at the outset at least, starts with how welcoming the space feels and how pleasant the receptionist is. We all know that feeling, arriving somewhere feeling anxious and then being welcomed and put at our ease by someone who greets us. Or, if the opposite is true, we know how off-putting it is. Waiting rooms set the tone for the therapy experience.

When we enter a waiting room, we immediately become aware of the sights, sounds and smells. The best spaces will offer respite for the exhausted and anxious: comfortable couches, magazines, perhaps even coffee, certainly water. The experience of sitting in the waiting room can be many things: isolating, frustrating, or boring. But it can also be calming. Perhaps, for some, there is even a sense of anticipation.

A 'waiting room' implies a state of passivity, even limbo. It is absolutely fine to use the waiting room for whatever we personally need the space to provide. Sometimes we need to flip through outdated copies of *Hello!* magazine, or doze, or scroll through a Facebook or Instagram feed, taking a mental break before we settle down to the mentally engaging business of seeing our therapist.

Despite the fact that clients spend only a brief time each week in the waiting room, they will often form some sort of relationship with each other there. It may take a long time to develop but clients with a regular appointment time may, for years, see the same person with the slot before them, emerging each week from the consultation room. There's an understanding. A familiarity. A nod. Perhaps a smile. It helps to relieve the pressure of the situation that some people will inevitably be feeling.

* * *

When Helen, a woman in her mid-twenties, finally entered my clinic on that Friday morning, my first impression was that she perfectly fitted the email description she'd given of herself in our earlier correspondence, a confidential email exchange in which she explained her current situation and why she wanted to see me. Helen appeared depressed, with low self-esteem.

She was pale. Her posture was a little bent over. She was without energy and not very talkative. She was a self-referred client who had phoned my secretary directly for an appointment. Now, she was late, but here she was.

It takes courage to walk into a stranger's office and start talking about personal thoughts and feelings. I try to make clients more comfortable about coming in for their first session by offering to talk with them on the phone first, or via email, as Helen had done. In her email she had complained of low self-esteem and feelings of worthlessness. She also had a pessimistic view of the future, telling me: 'I can't see anything ahead for me.'

She had told me that her depression first appeared years ago in her early teens and that she had suffered several recurrences since. She was taking an antidepressant prescribed by her GP but had never had any psychotherapy, until now. She told me that the medication had helped her but she didn't want to take drugs all her life so had decided to try to solve her problems by coming to see me.

She also explained in her email that her childhood had been very traumatic, but she had not elaborated. She mentioned that everything from her childhood was connected to bitter feelings. She lived with her father, a retired teacher. Her mother was dead, but she remembered her as being a happy and outgoing person.

* * *

Like any first meeting, that morning set the tone for therapy. There is so much that happens in the first session: we meet the person, listen to their story, give information, make an assessment and negotiate our future therapy sessions, should they want to continue. Of course, the nature and format of the first session varies considerably depending on the individual and factors such as culture, religion and age.

Having had clients from a variety of cultures come to see me over time, I've become more aware of the influences different cultures bring to the therapeutic process. Culture influences our expectations about how human interactions will occur. Culture influences how we understand health and healing. A simple example is the way people seek medical attention when they are physically ill. Based on people's culture, some individuals choose the help of medical professionals, while others may choose different options, such as homeopathic remedies, fasting or acupuncture.

While acknowledging the role that culture plays in people's lives, I never assume that everyone has the same life experience and narrative, even if some clients do share certain aspects of identity. Everyone has their place within a culture that encompasses ethnicity, including other social aspects like family cultures, academic cultures, workplace cultures, culture of femininity and masculinity, religious cultures, and so on. Of importance too are a client's spiritual and religious influences. All this information lives in the background during our sessions, to be drawn upon as necessary.

In the first session I usually explain to clients the meaning of our therapy. I usually say something like: 'Therapy is a chance to grow and reach a deeper understanding of yourself. In my experience I believe that while your pain may be rooted in your past, healing takes place in the present. We might examine the past to gain an understanding of your current issues, but primarily we focus on the here and now. Rather than delving deeper into the problem, we examine the limiting beliefs that keep you stuck. We look for strengths, resources and alternative solutions.'

And every therapy then begins with a story about what has brought the client to my therapy room. This opens a window into a rich collection of autobiographical memories and narratives that will come to define the focus and arc of our sessions.

* * *

I asked Helen to tell me more about her life story and especially her mother's death, which she had mentioned in her email. I wanted to find out more about that early trauma.

Helen told me that she was born in Brighton, where her family had lived for most of her life. One of her earliest traumas happened when she was about six years old, visiting Brighton beach with her mother on a bright Sunday afternoon. You can picture the scene. A cloudless blue sky, seagulls calling and the voices of children playing on the beach. A little girl skipping beside her mother, maybe rushing ahead in her eagerness to get to the beach.

Her mother, Helen told me, would usually sit on the pebbles while Helen would run to the edge of the sea, so that just her toes were submerged in the small wash. She would wave at her mother, and then run back. Helen's mother would give Helen a big hug. Then Helen would do it all over again. It's a lovely scene of precious time spent, mother with daughter.

'I suppose I thought she'd always be there for me to run back to,' Helen said. Her voice had lost the warmth it had contained when she was recounting her happy reminiscences. 'But that beach was where she abandoned me. She just left me alone on the beach while I was playing on the edge of the water. I'll never know how long I sat there before my father came to collect me.'

At the time, her father had offered an explanation for her mother's absence, and Helen had simply accepted it and gone home with him.

'I wasn't scared at the time,' she said. 'I was happy to go with my father. In my innocent child's mind, I had no reason to doubt him. It simply never occurred to me that my mother had left me for no reason.'

A mother deserting a child she is supposed to be protecting, leaving her in a public place and simply walking away, seeming not to care what happens to that small, vulnerable person, is a lot to take in.

'So when did you realise that your mother had abandoned you and was never coming back?' I had to ask.

Helen said she couldn't remember quite when it hit her that her mother wasn't coming back. It had been more of a slow realisation that things were different now because, as odd as it still seemed to her, after that day no one really mentioned her mother again. That must have been a very difficult thing for a child to comprehend, I suggest. Her mother, who had been the mainstay of her life, was now not even spoken about. She had returned home that day from the beach with her father and it was as if, suddenly, her mother simply didn't exist any more, just a vague story about her having gone to live with an uncle and not being entirely well.

Helen and her mother had often gone for walks and explored beaches and nearby villages together, so everywhere Helen went from then on reminded her of her mother. It was painful every time she went some-where and pictured how things had been, and how they now were. But for the months and years ahead, there was complete silence regarding her mother's disappearance, and if Helen dared raise the subject it was quickly changed.

Years later, when she was twelve, her father finally decided to tell her the truth about what had happened to her mother. She returned home from school on a Friday afternoon, just before the school Christmas holidays.

Helen started crying at this point. It was clear that it was difficult for her to talk about it and I told her to take her time, that there was no rush.

Eventually she continued, and I could hear the pain in her voice.

'I remember it was a very ordinary, bleak December day,' Helen told me. 'I sat on my father's left, so we were side by side. He spoke in a quiet, deep voice. I remember being restless; he was speaking in such a serious way it made me nervous. He was building up to something, but I remember not totally listening until he completed his speech with these words: "Helen, your mother is dead. She will never come back. She killed herself when you were six years old, after abandoning you on the beach."'

I asked Helen what she had said in response, and how she had felt.

She had been incredulous.

'I'd been told that my mother had left us and was living in Birmingham with her uncle and that she was unwell. I was promised, from time to time, that she would eventually return home … so when my father told me that my mother was dead, I actually remember that I burst out laughing.

My father started stroking my back with the palms of his hands, as you might comfort a baby. It was a soothing gesture. He said again that my mother had killed herself on the day she'd abandoned me on the beach. She had come back home and hanged herself in the dining room, while my father was in the garage cleaning his car. He had found her body and called for the police, who took her away. I remember my father's eyes went glassy when he said this, his mouth turned down and his brow knotted. It was like a cloud had passed over the sun, like a shadow had crossed his face. I remember I was still frozen in a smile. Then we both started weeping.'

I asked Helen what she remembered next.

'I remember my father making a noise, a long, single note of pain that still haunts me. It rang inside me and through me,' she said. 'I went to the bathroom. I remember swallowing a handful of painkillers, then I went to my bedroom and lay there looking up out of my window, my heart racing. I told myself this must be what dying felt like, that the pain would be gone, that it would all be over, that it was for the best. Dad kept popping in, his face showing his concern, to check I was OK. Eventually I passed out. I woke up the next day with a massive headache.'

Her response was hardly surprising; imagine the trauma of hearing something like that when you are twelve. When you had thought that your parent was simply elsewhere, in another part of the country.

That morning, she decided she did want to die; she just couldn't cope any more. She returned to the bathroom to take more tablets to kill herself. Her father had anticipated her actions and removed the painkillers.

* * *

Towards the end of the first session with a client, I will often try to ask them how they have experienced the session and how they've found talking with me. I asked Helen: 'You've said how hard it is to talk about your feelings and your mother's death, and yet you've talked a lot about your feelings here with me today. What has that been like for you?'

Relational reflections like this set the tone for therapy to come. Helen said that she'd found it very easy to talk and that she felt safe, and that's a pleasing response. I asked if there was anything else she wanted to say before we finished the session.

She looked thoughtful for a moment, then said: 'The strangest thing is that my mother was an extrovert. She was confident and quick to reach out and make friends. She used to work as a teacher and socialise with her colleagues. I just don't understand why she would kill herself.'

From a child's perspective this sort of juxtaposition can be difficult to rationalise. She saw her mother as confident, extrovert and happy but had then been forced to confront the stark truth that her mother must have been a very unhappy woman and that she, as her child, had not been enough to stop her mother from taking her own life.

The session with Helen reminded me of clients I had seen in the past who had survived suicide. Suicidal thoughts can sometimes be neatly camouflaged under big, brave smiles, beautiful multicoloured layers of jokes and shiny defence mechanisms. People who want to die are not always the shy introverts, or the ones in obvious pain and trauma.

We see this clearly when the media report stories of people who have taken their own lives and are seeking to provide a 'reason', to bring logic to the illogic of self-termination. This is particularly common when it comes to the suicides of celebrities, because the idea that someone who has achieved great worldly success but can still be miserable seems so unreasonable. A question we all have, when we hear someone famous and brilliant like Robin Williams has taken their own life, is why would a person with so much of what the rest of us want choose to end their life?

The danger of playing the 'looking for a reason' game is that we end up with the conclusion that the person must have been selfish or a coward, and these are explanations for someone taking their own life that I hear all too often in the media and indeed from individuals. Helen's mother, for example, didn't seem to suffer from a disastrous marriage, nor was she a hopeless addict. In my experience, most people who take their own life often have little 'reason' other than depression, and that—this terrible illness at the heart of so much tragedy—is reason enough. We are all prisoners of our own flawed brains and are prone to the same terrifying vulnerability that Helen's mother and celebrities like Robin Williams have experienced.

There is an exaggerated optimism that life is going to be somehow better and happier with more love, money and success. I'm not saying that money, love and success aren't important. Rather, this is a plea to acknowledge that there's more to life than money, success and, yes, love! In our culture, many of us idealise love. We see it as a lofty cure-all for life's problems. And because we idealise love, we overestimate it and, all too often, our relationships pay the price. When this happens we're more likely to ignore fundamental values such as respect, humility and commitment towards the people we care about. After all, if love solves everything, then why bother with all the other 'stuff' in life?

Love is a powerful word, possibly the most powerful and emotive word in the English language. But there is tremendous confusion about how to define it. Or maybe it is because of its scope and power that the definition of love seems to elude us. We all mean something specific, something that is unique to ourselves, when we speak of it. The thing is, it may not mean precisely the same thing to anyone else.

For me, personally, love means there is room in my relationship with others to be my whole self and that can be sometimes powerful, sometimes nurturing, sometimes broken, sometimes selfish and sometimes generous. And at the same time it allows room for another person's whole self to be part of my whole self. For the emotionally wounded who come to see me, it takes time to metabolise these feeling to create the space to become whole again. I know from having been a client myself, my attachment to my own therapist took many forms.

At the start of my sessions I needed my therapist like I needed gravity, to keep me oriented. At the time I didn't need to think much about how he felt about me. He displayed consistent interest in understanding me. That was enough. He didn't recoil as my emotional mess poured out all over his office. In time his consistency, patience, kindness and, yes, love helped me become whole again.

We live in a culture that's highly attuned to what's beautiful and moving about love; we know its high points and celebrate its ecstasies in films, songs, fairy tales and religion. To know love could be considered one of our most basic and fundamental needs.

I am thinking of pure love in its broadest sense, a love that goes beyond feelings for a particular person and can include love of our pets, our homes, aspects of nature, ideas, books, works of art. In contrast to the often fickle romantic love of infatuation that can disappear as quickly as it comes and can prove to be unhealthy, addictive or painful, pure love of the heart only enriches. As Scott Peck remarks in his book *The Road Less Traveled*: 'Love always requires courage and involves risk.'[7]

I believe that the majority of psychotherapists would agree that psychotherapy is all about love, particularly in longer-term therapy. What we mean by that is not so much that the explicit goal of therapy is to help our clients experience more love or to love better, although that is often the case. Rather we are referring to love as something that can be experienced by the client and the therapist in the psychotherapy relationship and as part of the psychotherapy process.

Clients come to see us in times of psychological distress, often as a consequence of feeling unlovable and rejected. Therefore, they yearn to know themselves again as capable of loving and being loved. Thus, our love towards our clients is based on a compassionate care for another human being and an illuminating heart-warming acknowledgement of

---

[7] Peck, M. S. (1978). *The Road Less Traveled: A New Psychology of Love, Traditional Values, and Spiritual Growth*. New York, NY: Simon & Schuster.

human frailties, complexities, and strengths that empower clients to face the helplessness of the unknown.

* * *

Helen arrived the following week for her second session. She started by wanting to explain that after our initial conversation she had felt like redecorating her bedroom in a brighter colour, perhaps yellow. She was keen to let me know that she felt positive about beginning her therapeutic process and that she wanted to make a physical change to the environment in which she had spent so much of her life feeling depressed.

I was happy for her, I told her. It was a sign of a new, fresh and positive beginning. But I also wanted to continue to explore the aftermath of how she'd felt after finding out about her mother's death when she was twelve. It is a particularly sensitive age at which to experience a parent's death and I wanted to know what effect it had had on her.

* * *

An adolescent's grief can be impacted by any number of things, depending on the young person's cognitive and emotional development, including, but not limited to, their unique relationship with the individual and how the individual died. Due to the developmental changes taking place within the adolescent their reaction to death is likely to be extremely intense. Teens may grieve very differently to a child or an adult and often do not fully comprehend the enduring consequences of a loved one's death. They also experience the intense emotions of bereavement in shorter episodes than adults, punctuated by periods during which they resume normal activities.

Sometimes denial can be a helpful coping mechanism for a teen, as it occasionally acts as a filter, letting in small amounts of information at a time. But an important part of the healing process in therapy is remembering. In a time in their life when, these days, trauma for most twelve year olds is a bad selfie, the trauma that Helen had experienced was off the scale.

Just bringing up the name of the person who died is an important way to give children and teens permission to share their thoughts, feelings and questions about the person who has died. They need to be allowed to remember the deceased in a way that is meaningful to them. Encouraging a child or teen to express and talk about their feelings is very important and this can be done simply by sharing feelings about and memories of the person who has died.

Therapists act as role models for how to work through grief. Children and teens will copy the coping skills of the adults in their lives. However, in cases of complicated grief, like the suicide of Helen's mother, it creates a much bigger sense of confusion because there is a social stigma and shame accompanying these deaths. This creates feelings of embarrassment that are then projected inwardly in the form of self-hatred. Often these young people feel lonely and isolated. They cannot grieve normally.

Children and teens often feel guilt, fear, abandonment or depression if grief for a loved one is further complicated by being unresolved. There are eight indicative complicated grief symptoms: 'longing and searching for the deceased, preoccupation with thoughts of the deceased, purpose-lessness and futility about the future, numbness and detachment from others, difficulty accepting the death, lost sense of security and control, and anger and bitterness over the death.'[8]

* * *

'Over the years, I almost pretended I'd never had a mother,' Helen told me. 'I didn't talk about her or acknowledge the fact that I missed her. I remember crying secretly.'

Sometimes, a bereaved young person can become involved in risky behaviours in an attempt to manage their grief and its associated emotions. By sixteen, Helen said, she had been arrested for underage drinking and smoking marijuana. She was having sex with men almost twice her age. She was angry and hurt by her mother's suicide and drowning her emotions in alcohol and drugs.

Helen told me: 'For many years I waded through depression and anxiety, grief and guilt. Just as I had done as a teen, I partied all night and told myself I was having fun, trying to free myself in all the wrong ways.'

---

[8] Melhem, N., Moritz, G., Walker, M., Shear, M., & Brent, D. (2007). Phenomenology and correlates of complicated grief in children and adolescents. *Journal of the American Academy of Child Adolescent Psychiatry, 46* (4): 493–499.

But her mother's abandonment was only a small part of the unusual story of how she had ended up as a depressed, anxious adult with no confidence.

'The worst thing about my mother leaving was that I felt so uncontrollably emotional,' Helen said. 'One minute you're positive, the next you're negative. One minute I was smiling, the next I was trying to hold back the tears because I saw, heard or smelled something that reminded me of her. But I think the worst thing about her suicide was not her actual death (we all die eventually), but the shame and blame it leaves to haunt those who are still alive, like it has me and my father. I think society has got much better about lessening the stigma of mental health conditions, but the shame is still there.'

Unfortunately, as Helen identified, it is true that there can be a great deal of shame when someone you love dies by suicide. People in the community hear rumours, make assumptions and judge not only the person who died but the people who loved that person.

'So, how did your father cope and how was your relationship with him after he told you about your mother's suicide?' I asked.

'He made good use of my mother's disappearance and death as an excuse for anything and everything,' Helen told me. 'He wasn't a bad man, but he became an alcoholic after my mother's death. He wasn't a violent drunk or an abusive drunk, he was just drunk and it ruined his life and mine. He started drinking heavily after my mother's death.'

And, of course, that affected the whole relationship.

Helen continued to explain that she always felt rather distant from her father because they never talked much. She said that she was afraid to talk to him because she didn't want to get angry around him about her mother's absence. She didn't think he was strong enough to handle it.

That's an interesting thought. How many of us have held back because we have felt that we might be the straw that breaks the camel's back? Helen told me that her father had never tried to talk to her and had never asked her how she felt about taking over some of her mother's roles in the house. When Helen was in her teens she became responsible for preparing dinner for her father and doing other domestic chores around the house. They simply didn't communicate about the situation.

She reported that this led to an emotionally distant relationship in which her father seemed to avoid facing his own feelings.

* * *

Although some people who take their own life have an identifiable mental health problem, such as clinical depression, others don't. Some talk about wanting or planning to kill themselves, or give other hints. However, others don't. The decision to do it might be made just hours, minutes or seconds before the act. When a person very suddenly and without warning takes their own life, there is no chance for others to anticipate or prepare for it. It is possible that the people around the individual have no clue that their loved one was even struggling. Often, they are blindsided and left completely off balance.

Every suicide, like every person, is different. Many are sparked by intense feelings of depression, anger, despair, hopelessness or panic. However, although a considerable proportion of suicide attempts are the result of sudden impulses, not all are impulsive in nature. There are certain behaviours that may be signs of a potential suicide risk: unusual or unexpected visits or calls to family and friends; saying goodbye to people as if they won't be seen again; feelings of worthlessness, and self-hatred; trying to get access to guns, pills or other objects that could be used in a suicide attempt. In my experience clients who exhibit these signs are often communicating their distress, hoping to get a response from the people around them. These are very useful red flags that shouldn't be ignored.

Helen didn't think that her father had known her mother was struggling.

The death of a loved one is always difficult, as many of us will know. Our reaction will be influenced by the circumstances of the death, particularly if it is sudden or accidental. Reactions are also influenced by our relationship with the person who has died. A loss due to suicide, as Helen experienced, can be among the most difficult losses to bear. After a suicide, survivors like Helen and her father are left with many unanswered questions; important pieces of the puzzle are missing. Not fully understanding why the person did it can be one of the hardest parts of being bereaved by suicide.

Survivors are desperate to create a narrative that will explain why their loved one took his or her life. They become private investigators, leaving no stone unturned, studying phone bills and their loved one's behaviours, and interviewing anyone who had contact with them—often to no avail.

Helen searched for clues in her mother's diary, which she'd begun when Helen was born, and tried to know her through the entries and to understand their relationship better. For a while, she collected every picture she could find of her mother, scanning her eyes for sadness. It's painful to imagine this search for answers in old photos but it would be almost impossible for a young person left with so many unanswered questions not to succumb to that urge.

As Helen got older she tried to find answers in other ways, from meeting with psychics, to ordering the police report from the day her mother died. But with every answer came more unanswered questions and nothing seemed to bring her any closer to an understanding of her mother's death.

The truth is there is never a satisfying answer that solves the unknown. Survivors relive events leading up to the death; the 'what ifs' haunt them. They live with the 'would haves, should haves and could haves', which cause much anxiety and guilt. I asked Helen if that sounded familiar and she recognised it immediately.

We paused our session when Helen started to cry. I could see that she felt panicked and had started to hyperventilate. She was feeling anxious. She told me that her neck was hurting. The physical pain seemed to be connected to the thoughts she'd been expressing. Physical pain was a common occurrence when she talked about her childhood.

I suggested that we slow things down. Helen sighed.

* * *

A sigh or deep breath in therapy often indicates discharge. By slowing Helen down, I was encouraging her to relax, allowing her nervous system to unwind and discharge tension. There was a lot happening in the session and Helen needed to think about just one thing at a time, to work on just one fragment of her experience at a time, before moving on to anything else.

The more information we access in therapy, the more overwhelmed we can feel. I wanted to help Helen to self-regulate and move away from the state of fear and anxiety that she had become accustomed to experiencing when talking about her past traumas.

In this process, we were trying to work on the edge of her nervous system, together with her thoughts and memories. This is also referred to as 'mindfulness'. In research, mindfulness is shown to use neural pathways in the brain that cause the nervous system to calm. The more these neural pathways are used, the stronger they become.

Using mindfulness we start to notice what happens in the body when anxiety is present and at the same time we create mindful techniques to help clients 'signal safety' to their nervous system. Clients report being able to slow down their reaction to stimuli, control their body's fear response (fight or flight), and increase their tolerance for discomfort over time.

Mindfulness strategies work to shift the way you think of negative thoughts, allowing you to see them for what they are: meaningless words that come and go. This shift in interpretation decreases the likelihood of a response to the thought being triggered.

An example to better understand this approach is if we imagine that thoughts are like a soundtrack to a film and further imagine that there are two identical scenes of a couple driving in their car in the middle of the night. In one version of this scene, upbeat music is playing, perhaps to suggest a romantic encounter. As viewers, we might anticipate that the couple are going to embark on a romance as they head towards their destination. Now imagine the same scene. Only, this time, the soundtrack is dark, ominous and depressing. Now, as viewers, we are anticipating that something unpleasant is going to happen to the couple. Mindfulness will help you to experience a scene as safe and happy even when the music prompt tells us otherwise. Mindfulness helps clients to learn to change their music.

* * *

I suggested to Helen that she might want to close her eyes, if it felt OK. I asked her if we could go back to that moment when she had had that creative impulse to decorate her bedroom: 'The moment that thought came to you,' I reminded her. 'Tell me about that and, then, how you created it. When you went into action. How you gathered materials and you created this beautiful place for yourself in your home. A newly decorated brightly coloured bedroom … Kind of like a womb or a safe "container".'

I asked Helen to just sit with the image of her new, positive bedroom and the experience of decorating it. I asked her if she was noticing anything at all in her body as she took herself back to her bedroom, and to the creation of it.

'Listen to your heart. Just take a moment and let me know … What are you sensing in your body, as you slow things down to just *be* in your body?'

Helen responded that her body felt good, that her torso felt warm—like the yellow colour she had used for her walls. I had helped her to locate her inner resources and to focus on the connection between the positive action of decorating her bedroom and her bodily sensation, particularly sensing all the love that Helen had given herself through this project.

With things slowed down, it was now possible to go back to my questioning.

* * *

The most traumatic and complex issue that a survivor must confront is: 'Why?' This is a topic that can plague them their whole lives. Even if there was a strong reason for the suicide, it is still intolerable in the eyes of those left behind that this was considered the only solution.

Suicide results from illness, and that illness is mental, psychological and emotional. Society's attitude to someone taking their own life means it is much easier to explain death from cancer or a road accident.

We must be wary of the expression 'committed suicide'. 'Committed' brings to mind something terribly wrong that someone has done wilfully, deliberately. Common synonyms for the word include: 'perpetrate', 'be to blame for', 'be guilty of' and 'to be responsible for'. Those who take their lives do not want to die, but they just can't bear to live in the incredible pain that their illness is causing them. It is best if we remember those who attempt or succeed in suicide beyond their depression, anxiety and suicidal death, because they too were people who were loved and are missed.

Imagine yourself as a child secure in the world that your parents have made for you, living life in the certainty that they will always be there to pick you up and kiss you better. The consequences of parental suicide are profound and unimaginable. It rips out a part of the child's persona and sets in motion a domino effect of emotions felt later on as an adult, often resulting in chaos. I wanted to explain to Helen the emotional consequences of parental suicide.

First, there is disbelief. Is this really happening to me? The person affected has difficulty comprehending reality, as if it's a dream, and there is an urge to wake up from the dreadful dream but to no avail. By losing hold of reality one stays in a transitional state, not knowing what to believe and what not to believe.

Second, there is disenchantment. Parents were once everything in the world to the child, but when one ceases to exist, it means the world around them stops.

The third emotional consequence is low self-esteem. This happens because deep down there is a belief that the deed was due to them, that he or she was the cause of such a dreadful act. The result is that one starts losing confidence.

Low self-esteem leads to indecisiveness and a narrow perspective of the universe. This creates a lens that alters clients' perceptions of the environment and, to a lesser or greater degree, alters everything they experience. Everything they encounter is contaminated by this negative prism. Their whole perception of truth and reality has been distorted.

When people describe depression as your mind lying to you, this is what they mean. Your mind is interpreting things as it understands them but, because of a negative mindset, this understanding is fundamentally flawed. This distortion is variable; sometimes things seem clear, sometimes things are significantly worse, but it's always there.

There's no way to see around the lens, so there's no way to see the truth beyond.

I explained these processes to Helen so that she could understand what she was going through and so that she could perhaps understand her father's grief and how her mother's suicide would have affected him.

When we talk about suicide, it is also helpful to examine it from the perspective of 'four givens'. First suggested by Irvin Yalom,[9] they are

---

[9] Yalom, I. D. (1989). *Love's Executioner and Other Tales of Psychotherapy*. New York: Basic Books.

called 'givens' because they are unavoidable. Death is one of those 'givens' and to be alive means having to resolve these 'givens' in some way:

- Death—How do we live knowing we are going to die?
- Freedom—How do we use the freedom we have to choose how we live our lives?
- Isolation—We are born alone, and we die alone. How do we reconcile our internal sense of 'aloneness' with our need for company?
- Meaninglessness—How do we make meaning in a universe which is essentially meaningless?

Although they may seem quite distinct, these 'givens' tie rather neatly into the first one: death. Yalom says that an innate fear of death is present at every level of human consciousness: from the most conscious and intellectualised, to the deepest depths of the unconscious, which manifests as death anxiety.

* * *

Following this initial assessment, Helen agreed that her main goal would be to process and come to terms with the trauma represented by her mother's suicide and abandonment. I used a traditional client-centred approach to help Helen deal with this trauma—which meant carefully reflecting Helen's narrative back to her, while facilitating her experiences of associated emotional states. This approach dominated the first ten weeks of therapy.

During the 1950s, humanistic treatments became popular in the United States. Carl Rogers suggested that counselling could be more straightforward, warm and hopeful than that provided by behavioural or psychodynamic psychologists. In contrast to psychodynamic and behavioural approaches, he believed that clients benefit from being motivated to reflect on their current subjective experience rather than any implicit intent or someone else's perception of the situation. Rogers concluded that therapists should be warm, sincere and understanding in order for a client's condition to change.[10]

---

[10] Rogers, C. (1951). *Client-centered Therapy: Its Current Practice, Implications and Theory*. London: Constable.

What Helen spoke about in this early phase of our work together tended to revolve around the initial trauma of her mother's suicide, her huge sense of loss, and her fear for the future. The initial shock of her father revealing to her that her mother was not coming back and that she had taken her own life when Helen was six had provoked a panic attack, and suicidal thoughts. She talked about her fear for the future and not being able to cope. To explain this, she described it as like being in a big lake, with sheer sides, only just able to breathe, but unable to get out of the lake on her own and needing somebody to throw her a life ring.

You can imagine the panic anyone would feel if they were trying to get out, feeling themselves sinking beneath the water with no help in sight. Helen needed somebody to show her how to get out of the situation she found herself in. She wanted somebody to tell her how to learn about and deal with what she'd lost.

* * *

For many people, the fear of death results in not fully living. And given that we are all going to die at some point, death anxiety is a normal part of the human experience. However, in his book *The Four Agreements*, Don Miguel Ruiz[11] writes about 'surrendering to the angel of death'. By this he means accepting the impermanence of everything. Nothing really ever belongs to us. It's all on loan and death can take it at any time. Death takes us out of our normal routine and reminds us of the temporariness of life.

By the fifth session, Helen's narrative was beginning to change. To me it seemed as though the emotional trauma was losing its raw edge, as though Helen had come to accept and acknowledge her difficult and painful feelings, having made a choice to stop struggling with something she had finally realised she couldn't control. In that session I employed an exercise, a simple process of reflection, to help Helen acknowledge her feelings.

I asked her to identify the emotion she was having, for example anger or sadness. I then gave her the following instruction: 'Close your eyes

---

[11] Ruiz, D. M. (1997). *The Four Agreements: A Practical Guide to Personal Freedom.* San Rafael, CA: Amber-Allen.

(if that feels safe) and imagine putting that emotion five feet in front of you. Imagine that for just a few minutes you are going to put it outside yourself so that you can look at it.' I then asked her to answer the following questions. If your emotion had a size, what size would it be? If your emotion had a shape, what shape would it be? If your emotion had a colour, what colour would it be?

I then completed the exercise with the following statement: 'Once you've answered these questions, imagine the emotion out in front of you with the size, shape and colour you gave it. Just watch it for a few moments and recognise it for what it is. When you are ready, you can let the emotion return to its original place inside you.'

When we had finished with the exercise I asked Helen to reflect on what she'd noticed about her experience. I asked her the following questions: 'Did you notice any change in the emotion when you got a little distance from it? What about changes in your reactions to the emotion? What size, shape and colour did you give the emotion? Did the emotion feel different in some way once the exercise was finished?'

This exercise is based on Acceptance and Commitment Therapy, which has been shown to effectively treat a variety of psychological disorders. By employing it, Helen was hearing other aspects of her story being reflected back to her, and this opportunity to look again at what had happened to her brought other feelings to the fore. She began to re-evaluate the difficult relationship she had, over a number of years, with her father. We were making progress.

* * *

However, her story was about to become more emotionally complicated as there were further revelations to come. In the tenth month of our weekly meetings, Helen started her session with a new piece of information.

'I wanted to tell you something about my father. He has been keeping the truth about my mother's suicide away from me. Last Saturday when I went to visit him, he was drunk as usual and he said to me: "Your mother was not your real mother."'

I was surprised. Now imagine the shock for Helen. First she'd experienced the shock of losing her mother and all the complicated feelings that had created. Now she was hearing for the first time that her mother was not her real, or biological, mother. She continued to speak.

'I sat still, trying to absorb the shock. I felt sick. My whole life had been a lie. It was horrendous. My father handed me an envelope as he told me my mother's real name was Dorothy. Inside was a letter in strangely familiar handwriting, handwriting I almost share, and a photograph of a woman holding a small baby.'

Helen told me that, as the truth unfolded, she had felt no anger. Her initial feeling was one of sadness for her father, for having held on to this weighty secret for so long.

The letter very simply introduced her mother and said that she loved Helen, asking Helen to forgive her for not being with her as she had breast cancer and was dying. The letter was only one paragraph and Helen found out that her mother had written it shortly before passing away in hospital when Helen was very small.

Her father told Helen that the nurse who had taken care of Dorothy became her adoptive mother. She and Helen's father had started a relationship soon after her biological mother's death. They had eventually married and Helen's adoptive mother had raised her as her own daughter.

Over the next few weeks Helen tried to find out more about her biological mother. Her father had given her details of relatives she could contact. She found a cousin who agreed to meet her. When he produced a box with four or five photos of her mother, she was speechless. There she was, smiling and laughing. Another of her relatives she found remembered her mother as a larger-than-life person, always smiling. This was something Helen liked to hear.

'How do you feel about your adoptive mother now?' I asked Helen.

'I don't think my father ever intended to tell me the truth,' she said. 'I asked him why he didn't tell me before and he said it was because I was a sensitive child and he didn't want to upset me, as I was already psychologically scarred by her abandonment and suicide. When I asked him why he didn't tell me, even in adulthood, he said he had given my mother, who had died when I was ten months old, a deathbed promise to keep the secret. I didn't believe him and I think the real reason was the fear that I might abandon him as well.'

I told Helen that I thought it was highly unlikely that her mother would have said this; the suggestion being that her father had lied to her.

I explained that in many instances lying represents the path of least resistance. Parents are also human and when they feel they can outsmart others and get away with it pretty easily they will do it more often than not, especially when dealing with children. Lying can also save us from admitting our wrongs and the need to offer apology. Admitting to being wrong or to doing wrong is not an easy thing to do. Perhaps the embarrassment of having a relationship with someone so soon after Helen's mother Dorothy had died was too embarrassing and emotionally taxing for Helen's father.

In the last few months Helen had decided to try to have a better relationship with her birth family, the uncle and cousin she had contacted. I wanted to know what it had been like meeting some of her biological relatives. But it seemed that the experience hadn't been positive. She had wanted to find out more about her mother but found only that these people were strangers to her. She would hear stories of their childhoods and her mother's, and listen to their memories, and it meant nothing to her. The good, the bad—she had had no part in it. How disappointing, and Helen had probably hoped so much that this would be a vital link to her past.

So what had she learned? Certainly she had found an explanation for why she had never really felt connected to anyone. Her missing heritage, not knowing where she really came from, meant that she had never had any real sense of belonging. Now there was an explanation for this, she thought. I wanted to point out that there were positives to be taken away, too. I asked if there was any resemblance between her and her biological mother.

Helen was quick to acknowledge that she had seen a similarity. 'I now know where I get my physical appearance from. It's good to know, or at least to see, the physical reflection of your genetics in another person. It's something that I grew up never having, but now that I've experienced it, I would never trade it for the world. That moment when you first see someone else, someone who has your cheekbones, your eyes, your chin—other than when you see yourself in a mirror—it's amazing! Now I know there was someone else in the world like me. Now I know who that person is. I know where I fit on this planet and I don't feel so lost, so out of place any more.'

There was a new philosophy to her thinking.

'I guess the parents who raise you are your parents, even though my "mother" killed herself when I was six. And the relatives that you know growing up are all "related" to you. But beyond that there's nothing; I feel zero connection to "great-great grandmother So-and-So" who has no blood relationship to me whatsoever. Those ancestors belong to my parents and cousins, but not to me. I guess it's the complete opposite with my birth family. With them, although I have just discovered them, I do not feel that they are *my* cousins, uncles, etc. Not in the sense that I feel that way about the family I grew up with. They are strangers who are related to me by blood, but with whom I have no shared history. Yet when they talk about our mutual "great-great grandmother So-and-So", then I *do* feel connected. The same blood that ties them to our ancestors ties me as well. But somehow I don't feel like a child "belonging" to one parent or the other. I feel caught in the middle.'

Helen had identified an emotional bond that was stronger with her non-biological family, and was concerned that perhaps that was wrong. I explained to Helen that it takes much more than DNA to bond people together. There are many people who have close family relationships with those who are not their blood relatives and, likewise, there are families who are related by blood who don't get along at all. Our DNA does not manifest the emotional attachment that a person would. It's the mind and the heart that are responsible for the feelings of love for a person.

I don't think that biology is the most important aspect of the foundation of the family. Some argue that the biological tie is essential to parenthood. However, adoptive parents and step-parents have the same rights and obligations as biological parents. A mother or father is someone who takes care of a child, comforts, gives advice, loves unconditionally, and the list goes on.

A parent is one who grows a strong relationship with the child and most importantly is always there for the child. Once you have that connection with each other it doesn't matter whether you conceived the child or not, especially if the biological parent is not involved in the child's life. A 'real parent' can be anyone who takes on the responsibilities of parenting and provides the love.

* * *

At the core of adoption there is always the issue of biological bonds versus psychological bonds. Adoption makes the normal developmental stages more complex, particularly in regard to issues of attachment and loss. In Helen's case it gets more complicated because her non-biological mother took her own life when she was six and her biological mother died from cancer when she was a baby. And, with Helen, the issue is not merely that it is painful for her, but also that it was painful for her father.

Her emotions included loss and grief, and feelings of guilt, shame and inadequacy, which have had a disturbing influence on her self-image and identity. She has experienced a sense of loss of control, feelings of rejection, and the continuing fear of further rejection, isolation and alienation. Helen had been dealt two hammer blows before she was even in double digits. It was a poor beginning. Throughout her life she has suffered from lowered self-esteem and unresolved grief. All of which makes the therapy process challenging.

Many adoptees like Helen experience a lifelong fear of abandonment and rejection, along with feelings of not belonging, and of being powerless over what has happened in their lives. These feelings don't stem from the adoption per se, but from the relinquishment that came before it. In order for Helen to move on with her life her losses needed to be recognised and mourned.

My first task, then, was to help Helen to differentiate between bonding and attachment, motherhood and parenthood. This would help make distinct the nature of Helen's relationships with her birth mother and adoptive mother, and minimise the sense of divided loyalties.

Effective therapy in this case requires the capacity to create an environment sufficient to hold and express the multiple and often disparate meanings attached to what happened in Helen's life experiences.

Bonding, I told Helen, is the complex physiological and psychological tie between a mother and her child that develops through pregnancy, and exists from then on. The strength of this birth bond is one of the factors that later draws children, like Helen, into a search to find out more about their birth parent. Attachment, which is the result of nurture, develops between parent and child during the early years, and defines the bond in an adoptive family—just as it did with Helen's non-biological mother until Helen was six.

So much of childhood is defined by how we position ourselves in relation to our parents, how they go from seemingly omnipotent super-beings to our super-cool, super-smart landlords, to people we can't stand to be around, to real, live human beings with flaws and strengths like anybody else. Our parents loom large in our lives. What, then, Helen wanted to know, had been the likely influence of having and losing two mothers? And what lasting effect had Helen's father had on her?

The truth is, as research suggests, our parents' parenting methods have no noticeable effect on our permanent personality traits. Freud's big idea was that parents play a defining role in shaping the personalities and emotional health of their children. He also introduced the idea that parents, through influencing a child's unconscious, could actually shape how a child sees him or herself and how they see the world. Intuitively it makes sense. However, research with hundreds of pairs of twins, separated at birth, concludes that around 45 per cent of our personalities and behavioural patterns are based on genetics; the other 55 per cent are based on our environment, life circumstances, and life histories.

This means that we more or less end up who we are regardless of who is parenting us. Put another way, our parents determine the superficial stuff like what sports team we like, how we like to dress, where we hang out, but they don't determine the important stuff—self-esteem, sexuality, introversion or extroversion, neuroticism, political views and so on. Mum and Dad are actually just one part of a larger equation.

* * *

Helen understood what I was saying, but still didn't know what to do with her feelings of guilt. She still felt responsible for her mother's death. 'I feel that if I had told her on that day on the beach to stay or perhaps if I hadn't run away to the edge of the water, she would've stayed with me.'

Helen's guilt was a means of expressing how fervently she wished to have her non-biological mother with her still. Dismissing guilty feelings won't stop the grieving person from feeling blame and may lead to the increase of these feelings. So, instead of dismissing her feelings, I gently urged her to express her sorrow and guilt further.

Being aware of her grief reaction and encouraging Helen to express herself is the essential first step in helping her—or someone in similar circumstances—to normalise the experience. Giving permission to talk is a key strategy in grief therapy. In my experience clients need to tell their story of loss more times than the people in their life want to hear it. This process of accepting a client's emotional outpourings without censoring them is part of their grieving and healing process.

I also encouraged Helen to take on small, everyday tasks such as walking to the shops, or posting the mail, in order to get out of the house, even for a little while. Known as graded task assignments, for many people these short-term approaches to dealing with grief and depression lay the groundwork for eventual healing and recovery. For some, these approaches also connect to a broader sense of purpose. Setting specific goals for each day or for the week is a useful way of staying organised and productive.

Helen undertook these small but important tasks reluctantly, with concerns about trying to 'put on a brave face' in public. She related a particular incident where she was at the local shop. When picking items from the shelves, she had instinctively selected her mother's favourite brand of tea. Feelings of panic had swept over her as she realised that she didn't need to buy the tea at all, but she couldn't bring herself to return it to the shelf. In this state, she left all her purchases in the shop and walked straight home.

This incident had increased Helen's anxiety about her ability to cope and to accept her mother's death. When she told me about it, I validated Helen's experience as being a normal and legitimate part of her grieving.

As a part of the therapeutic process, I needed to clarify and identify the causes and effects of Helen's feelings of panic. Although she had now fully accepted that her mother's absence was causing her anxiety, a belief that she would never be able to accept her mother's loss was also causing a fear of losing control in public places. By discussing the nature of her anxious feelings, and her associated beliefs and fears, together we devised a number of goals, including the development of new beliefs, relaxation and the simple act of taking it one step at a time.

Helen was able to say herself: it is normal to want my mother back; it's normal to grieve for and miss my mother; it doesn't matter if I cry in public and time will help me to heal. She kept notes in a personal journal about when she used these new beliefs. Journal writing was a process that allowed her to identify other problematic beliefs and thoughts.

Once she'd identified them, she was able to develop more appropriate and accepting beliefs.

Helen's increasing acceptance of the loss of her mother became more obvious with the passing of time. After twelve months of our sessions, the rewards for Helen were evident in her long-term improvement and growth. Her ability to develop goals for herself was greatly improved, as was her motivation.

After two years in therapy dealing with her despair and grief, she naturally moved on with her life and mourned less and less. She began to live independently again, away from her father, and she took on more responsibility. She began to make plans for her life without the approval of others, plans which included a number of support mechanisms, as well as long-term goals.

Social and emotional support for clients can result from a wide variety of sources—family members, friends, close acquaintances or peers. These support systems can give us advice, help us to learn new skills, keep us on the right track and hold us accountable to do what needs to be done.

Helen also expressed an interest in honouring both of her mothers by writing a book. She wanted to combine her own journal and both of her mothers' journals to recount the significance of their lives and deaths. The process would be a means to resolve her grief and offer a parting gift to her dead mothers. While Helen accepted that she would never completely 'get over' their deaths, she was able to accept that that was OK. She was able to come to the conclusion that both of her mothers would remain a part of her forever.

Additional thoughts

The death of a loved one will impact each of us differently, and will also depend on our previous relationships. For example, it is particularly difficult to raise a child through adolescence if their older brother or sister killed themselves. I have not contemplated taking my own life but I understand the dark forces that can drive a person to it.

Suicide is a complicated thing. Whatever the motive, whatever the unfathomable darkness that stirs within us, there is no doubt that it will generate catastrophic effect on the family left behind. The questions that cannot be unfolded, the guilt, the anger, the disintegration, destruction—there are simply not enough words to say how devastating it is.

Suicides are, in fact, often preventable. More often than not, people who are deeply depressed and have thoughts of suicide don't tell anyone. But in my experience, those who willingly tell other people about their suicidal thoughts are usually sharing the responsibility of their anguish and are crying for help.

It is normal to be afraid of death but death anxiety becomes abnormal when it forms the basis of pathological thoughts and behaviours that interfere with normal living. As therapists we know that death anxiety is related to a number of anxiety disorders including specific phobias, social anxiety, panic disorder, agoraphobia, post-traumatic stress disorder and obsessive compulsive disorders.

For example, when children experience separation anxiety disorder, it is often connected to excessive fear of losing major attachment figures (such as parents or other family members), to harm or tragedy from car accidents or significant illness, or when seeing clients with OCD (obsessive compulsive disorders) who repeatedly check stoves and locks in an attempt to prevent harm or death. Finally, specific phobias are characterised by excessive fears of heights, spiders, snakes and blood—all of which are driven by death anxiety.

There is also a specific phobia called thanatophobia or fear of death. Thanatophobia is an unusual or abnormal fear of personally dying and/or being dead that impacts the otherwise 'normal' or healthy functioning of the person possessing this fear that might appear disproportionate to an outsider relative to the actual risk or threat the individual faces.

In many Buddhist traditions, a purposeful contemplation of death is one practice that is used to help individuals become aware of the constancy of change and life's fragility. This concept suggests that when we realise that nothing in life is permanent and everything is easily broken, we look at events in our lives differently. We may appreciate to a greater level not only what we have (including health, relationships and possessions), but also the people we love.

From this perspective, while we may grieve loss (from the breaking of a favourite cup to the loss of something greater), we understand it to be part of a greater whole.

Archbishop Desmond Tutu, who won the 1984 Nobel Prize for his role in the anti-apartheid movement in South Africa, once said: 'When you have a potentially terminal disease, it concentrates the mind wonderfully. It gives a new intensity to life. You discover how many things you have taken for granted—the love of your spouse, the Beethoven symphony, the dew on the rose, the laughter on the face of your grandchild.'

Death is both certain and uncertain. We know it will happen, but we don't know when. One of my friends who is a wonderful psychiatrist passed away earlier this year. It took me by surprise. I was just taking in his recent cancer diagnosis. The prognosis didn't look good, but death moved even faster. Losing a friend hurts deeply. But it's irreversible. When I miss him, I feel sad, but it also reminds me to celebrate life.

When death knocks on your door, be ready to leave and live without regrets. Let's not hold onto life as if it's permanent because it can blind our spirituality. We can't control how *long* we live, but we can manage *how* we live. For most of us, this is a very difficult thing to do. But we can do it, albeit imperfectly. We need to surrender to the fact that death, like life, is messy, unpredictable, scary and challenging. And if we come to terms with it, another fact is that each of us will make the journey in the best way we know how.

FOUR

John and Alice

Once a week, usually on a Saturday morning having just woken up like a tousle-haired sheepdog, puffy-eyed and discombobulated, I visit my local coffee shop and sit on my own in a comfy chair, listening to my favourite jazz album by Charles Lloyd—*Fish Out of Water*—while I reflect on the week's happenings.

I would like to be able to concentrate better at home, but for some things, I just need to be at a coffee shop. The distractions at home are far more time-consuming than anything I encounter here, maybe because they are none of my business! But it also depends on what I'm doing.

If I'm working on something I like but it isn't going very well, I need a more significant distraction to let my mind wander. This usually helps me settle whatever was bothering me. If I'm working on something I need to just hammer out, then I'll go to a coffee shop because I feel more motivated to stay put and work.

What I love to do most when I am there is write. I am aware that not all writers have to drink their favourite coffee when they write. Some writers need complete silence. Some need music. Some like watching TV shows as background noise. Coffee shops for me are good as a place to wind down and surround myself with the natural ambience of people chatting, clinking cups, and the espresso machine hissing. For me, that is what's calming.

* * *

However, on this particular Saturday morning, it was a much-needed day away from the usual clinical surroundings and thoughts with something familiar—my cappuccino and a piece of my favourite cake (chocolate Guinness cake). I know life can be very complicated at times but with my coffee in hand and a forkful of that delicious cake, I was feeling very mellow. But nevertheless, I do know there will always be curve balls to accommodate and adaptability to employ.

As I enjoyed my cake, I thought that as complicated as life can be, when it comes to relationships, those complications can multiply considerably.

Couples will often think of therapy as a way of addressing the problems they have, but in my experience there are as many different reasons for seeking therapy as there are couples looking for help.

I had been working on a rather complex case for the past six months and on that particular Saturday morning, I needed a respite. Among the most contentious issues with couples are those that involve an infidelity. A betrayal. Adultery. Cheating. Whatever name you choose for the emotional turmoil that follows.

When one partner finds out that the other has been cheating, it is like throwing a huge rock into a calm pond and watching the resulting ripples spread out from the centre. The ripples represent the accusations and the surfacing of many deep-seated resentments.

There are many reasons why a person might betray the trust of their partner and have an affair. Most often, it will be a complex situation that will vary from individual to individual. A lot of what goes on will depend on the circumstances of the person, their needs as an individual and, of course, the state of the relationship.

As psychologists we are in a privileged position. When we work with groups or with individuals, we get a peek into the window of their unconscious mind. When couples come to therapy, they are trying to find out what has happened within their relationship that they can put right. Along this road to discovery there will be several options to be considered. Included in those considerations will necessarily be separation and divorce. The process of rebuilding love and trust and emotional security is a long and painstaking task. Sometimes, couples find it simply is not possible. It can be a long and torturous process to re-establish the trust, the love and the emotional security that has been lost.

When a couple comes to me for the first time, I try not to rush to judgement solely on what I actually see and what they tell me. This is because when it comes to using the tools of psychotherapy, I strongly favour treatments that are evidence-based. As mental health practitioners we use different treatment approaches to help clients who are experiencing mental health issues to feel empowered and mentally strong again. Some of our treatment approaches have a strong grounding in scientific evidence and other treatments have less evidence supporting them. If the treatments we use have scientific evidence supporting the effectiveness of the treatments, they are called evidence-based treatments (EBTs).

That is not to say I think that all the answers will conveniently follow a manual. Life is just not like that. And some problems that clients have don't appear in any manual I've ever seen! That means my approach to treatment has to be adapted and tailor-made to the individuals who come to see me. This will usually be arrived at through personal development in teaching and clinical practice. Of course, my own intuition and experience will also sometimes let me sense that 'something is not right'. This will be a feeling I can't quite put my finger on, but it exists nonetheless. It will be because in my unconscious I sense something from the individual or couple in front of me. Intuition.

I need to assess emotional responses in combination with conscious feelings so that I can make better decisions. Carl Jung defined intuition as a function of the psyche that gives insight and outlook on a situation. Some people will call this intuition a 'gut feeling' or something that is merely sensed. People often speak about intuition as being a gift or even a way of seeing into the future. In actual fact, every one of us has intuition.

As humans, that intuition can also be instrumental to our survival. Intuition is the instinct that warns us of imminent danger, when it would be dangerous to cross the road for example, or the feeling that something is not quite right. The culture we live in has taught us to rely on the five senses of sight, hearing, taste, touch and smell. In fact, intuition plays just as important a role. Not only in our survival, but also as an essential to our psychological and emotional well-being.

Psychologists at the University of New South Wales in Australia ran a series of experiments in 2016 in which they tried to quantify intuition. They did an analysis of how much emotional information received in a non-conscious form actually influenced decision-making. This study was very interesting because it found that as well as increasing the accuracy of predicting outcome, we also become more adept at using our intuition over time, much in the same way as we use reason or logic.

* * *

I remember one piece of advice given to me on this subject that over time has proved invaluable. My supervisor gave the advice to me at a time when I was wrestling with what would be the best therapy approach for a married couple. I guess one reason for my hesitation was that even in my earlier years of NHS clinical placement, couples coming to me for therapy produced reactions ranging from unease to severe anxiety.

My training initially had been entirely with individuals; and I was only just starting to train with couples. I found at the time that the theoretical books we used gave no real practical help with couples counselling. Fortunately, I was placed with a supervisor who had also trained in couples therapy and introduced me to a variety of psychotherapeutic approaches. As I puzzled over the best way forward with this particular couple my supervisor said, 'Just go with your professional gut and put your trust in your instincts.'

* * *

At the time that John and Alice came to see me they had been married six years. They met at university and were both now working as lecturers at the same institution. John was teaching mathematics and Alice was teaching history. Both of them were very academic and had envisaged improving their lot to make their lives happier and healthier than their parents' lives.

They had a very intelligent approach to each other, recognising each other's talents and listening, understanding and supporting each other. Importantly they both shared the same vision for their lives. They were both practising Christians.

However, their relationship had suffered a shift when, a month earlier, John discovered two used condoms next to the marital bed on the side where Alice slept. Alice had been on the pill for some time and as a couple they had not used condoms during the six years they had been married. Naturally enough John wondered what the used condoms were doing on the floor beside Alice's side of the bed. John confronted Alice but she vigorously denied ever seeing the condoms before that moment.

John had trouble believing this and was convinced that Alice was cheating on him. Alice countered this accusation by accusing John of doing the cheating, and, now that the condoms had been discovered, trying to frame her so he would have an excuse to leave her. At that point John got angry and was moving his head back and forth, like a raging bull, as though he wanted to hit her. They started hitting out at each other. Things got worse when Alice tried to grab the bedside lamp to hit him with and John gripped the lamp she was holding, drew back and the lamp knocked into his face. The light bulb broke, cutting Johns cheek. Blood was everywhere. It was splattered all over the bedroom floor. Alice was at a stage where she didn't care any more about anything, especially John.

They decided, eventually, that they needed to see a therapist as they were getting nowhere and the arguments between them were escalating. It was always the same question: who had put the used condoms on the floor next to Alice's side bed, and why? Alice found herself getting more and more depressed.

A colleague of mine worked at the same academic institution. Knowing both John and Alice and aware of their relationship struggles but not privy to the details, this colleague recommended me to them for therapeutic help. They both agreed to contact me. And that is how they arrived at my clinic.

* * *

As I considered this case I came to realise it was going to take all of my skill to confront this couple on the issues that would need to be addressed to untangle the struggle between them. I could not fathom what logical reason there could be for the condoms to appear on Alice's side of the bed that morning as both were denying responsibility. I felt very confused about the whole issue. I did, however, trust my 'gut feeling'. And that was telling me that both Alice and John were being truthful.

There is often conflict in couples therapy just by the very nature of the fact that the couple concerned has issues. From a therapist's point of view I had to ask myself how I could speak to a partner who's been betrayed and has stayed in that victim's role for a long time after the initial infidelity has been discovered. My worry was that I might say something that the couple would not agree with and there might be also the chance that there was no victim in this relationship. I certainly did not want to antagonise them. My hesitation was due to the fact that there were no clear signs as to who was the victim.

Eventually I realised there was nothing else for it but to confront each of them in turn and try to get to the bottom of what exactly happened with the condoms on that morning. My challenge was to manage the anger and hurt that was keeping the partner who saw himself or herself as having been deceived, in limbo, and unable to move on.

The next time I saw John and Alice, to my astonishment, they both told me that John had found another pair of used condoms! This time the condoms were not by the bed but were dangling from Alice's underwear on a chair. Alice, when confronted, had apparently been shocked once again and said she had no idea how the condoms had ended up on her underwear.

As Alice listened, I asked John to explain exactly what had happened this time.

John told me: 'Last Monday I woke up to find a pair of used condoms that were hanging from the front of Alice's underpants. It was obvious to me that she'd had sex with someone, quite likely when I was sleeping. As far as I can see this is the only possible explanation but Alice of course is denying it.'

Alice was very quick to respond to John's accusation and shouted: 'You're a big fucking liar! I'm disgusted in myself that I married a person who is so insecure. I can't believe I married such an anxious person! I deserve better!'

Alice was on her feet now, screaming in John's face.

It was a very stormy session, with Alice slamming out of the room only to return just before the end of the session. I was really quite surprised when she apologised to John.

Quite often, when you have to deal with this type of conflict between couples, you need to be fairly forceful because very often they will try to shout over each other and over you and that usually makes the session very difficult to manage successfully. Couples therapy is like walking through a minefield—take the wrong step and you can blow everything into a thousand pieces! However, this is about practice not perfection.

* * *

My method of managing these types of situations involves entering the argument on both partners' side and trying to get them to develop their argument more coherently, rather than pointing out the counterproductive things that they're saying and doing. The reason I want them to develop their arguments and articulate better what they want to say is because anger will typically be a fallback position.

When a couple fight, emotions run high and neither one can express what they want to say properly. Often in this kind of situation, even if you can express what you want to say, you're frustrated by the fact that your partner is not listening. If I am refereeing such a situation, I will try to get each partner to give the other a chance to speak and if that doesn't work, I will have to see each one individually.

In this case I explained to John and Alice that I needed to see them separately in individual sessions to get them to open up and reach a level of honest discussion that may not be possible if they were in the room together. I employ a three-step approach when I'm faced with couples in conflict:

1. I try to help them clarify and express what they want to say
2. I help them to listen to what their partner is trying to say (often after a few one-on-one sessions with me)
3. I create a platform on which they can both speak and be heard so that the analysis can move forward.

Since we first met, John and Alice had hardly been speaking to each other. If they did talk, it soon turned into an argument with Alice going to the bedroom, slamming the door behind her and crying on the bed. In these situations John would normally walk out of their house and drive over to his parents' home. Alice explained that almost a year before the therapy sessions with me she had begun to feel distant from John and isolated. She said that there was a lack of intimacy in the relationship and sex was now rare and that even cuddling with him seemed to be an effort.

Six sessions later it was clear to me that both John and Alice were suffering greatly under the strain. This was no surprise because one of the reasons that we react so badly when we are cheated on is that it has a profound impact on mental health and will cause greatly increased anxiety, depression and many other forms of distress.

* * *

Looking at the causes of this psychological distress there are several elements that make up the body blow to our mental health.

They will be:

- The fear of abandonment
- The feeling of losing control
- A feeling of low self-esteem
- The shock of a broken trust.

Even applying all that I knew to this situation, my gut feeling was telling me that there was something wrong and that despite John's certainty I was not at all sure that Alice was cheating on him.

As a therapist you often find yourself having to be an emotional detective as you try to coax your clients into telling you what they really hope to achieve from their therapy.

There are several important factors that every psychotherapist will have to keep in mind when working with clients. Some of those factors will be defined by the clinical training and the theoretical orientation we have, while other factors will be made up of the experience we have had in various clinical settings.

There are some essential tenets that apply in all areas of psychotherapy where the relationship eventually moves to a point where a client feels free to tell the story and express their frustration and pain. As they do this, the therapist becomes a container for the client's emotional outpouring and language. By language, I mean more than mere words. Non-verbal communication is key to the quality of the relationships we have.

* * *

Another important factor is that of sensitivity. We often use the word sensitivity to describe the sensations we feel in hearing, taste, touch and so on. But by the same token human beings also have varying degrees of emotional sensitivity. Some clients are more emotionally sensitive than others. Clients with greater emotional sensitivity can sometimes tell what those with less sensitivity are feeling before they know it themselves. This can be unsettling in a conversation, if not handled properly.

People with high emotional sensitivity seem to grasp, intuitively, how other people are feeling, coping, etc. Conversely, a person with low emotional sensitivity can sometimes have a really hard time intuitively understanding what another person is feeling. This person may need a lot more explaining to and more direct and specific requests in order to be emotionally supportive and responsive.

Low emotional sensitivity may make a spouse or partner feel misunderstood, or even lead them to believe (incorrectly) that the other person doesn't care about them. We're all familiar with the word "body language," and things like eye contact, a casual touch, voice tone, stance, and body movement all contribute to our non-verbal communication with others. Even when I was training I remember struggling to work up much enthusiasm for modelling and theories of behaviour.

Instead of that I try to 'feel' body language and to teach myself to actually 'hear' what's behind the stories and pain that I am hearing from my clients. I would help people to recognise certain words that may be a window onto the cause of the pain. Without saying a word you can communicate a whole range of feelings by just looking at someone: affection, attraction, interest, and even hostility can be conveyed in a single glance.

Holding eye contact is also a very important way of keeping the conversation going because as you keep eye contact with them you can gauge the response to what you're saying, and they can gauge your response as well. There is no doubt that non-verbal communication in psychotherapy is equally as important as any other method of communication.

Although non-verbal and verbal communication are actually the opposite of each other, there is no doubt that together they have synergy. This subject has been endlessly researched and findings are that, roughly, non-verbal communication accounts for 90 per cent and verbal communication only 10 per cent.

As therapists we also use the terms explicit and implicit communication to describe these two systems of 'language'—explicit communication is transmitted via spoken language and implicit via physical communication. It is also important to mention that non-verbal communication includes how loud and fast a client speaks or if they take any long or short pauses when they communicate verbally.

For example, clients can use what we call paralanguage and prosody in their mode of communication.

Prosody is the rhythm, stress, and intonation of speech that provides important information beyond a sentence's literal meaning. Prosody provides clues about attitude or effective state. The sentence 'It was great meeting with my boss,' can mean that the client liked the meeting with her boss or the exact opposite, depending on the client's intonation.

Paralanguage is the vocal features that accompany speech and contribute to communication. Paralanguage includes sounds such as ums, ahs, sniffs, sighs, gasps and shrieks. These sounds convey emotions in their intonation, pitch and rhythm.

Proxemics is another element that deals with the perception of space an individual has. (How much space do they take up personally? Do they sprawl or are they scrunched up in the corner?) For example, a commuter, used to being squashed into a train carriage every day, would see their space very differently to a farmer who spends all day on their own in the open air.

The other element of proxemics is the distance we feel we need to be from each other. (At this time of the Covid-19 pandemic, this distance is very much prescribed.) Each person has their own perspective of proxemics as it applies to them and very often clients will need a safe space to be in to help them find the words to explain their experience to their therapist.

In the case of John and Alice, I found that some of the subtle non-verbal communication and their expressions were leading me to the fact that Alice's disturbing behaviour and psychological condition was part of something that was underlying and very likely extremely complex.

* * *

It is difficult sometimes, as therapists, to remain entirely impartial during a therapy session. What I mean by this is that I have to be conscious that when I'm dealing with a heterosexual couple and I am one of the two men in the room, my female client does not feel threatened by this.

I suppose we have to be careful of the possibility of favouring one client over the other even in an unconscious way. If I am aware of this possibility then there is little chance for me to become biased towards one client over the other. This will ultimately be a positive influence for my clients, creating a therapeutic relationship which is unbiased and making our sessions better prepared for therapy.

We decided between us that the best thing to do would be for Alice to see me for individual sessions so that she could express her emotions without the risk that she would flare up and start shouting and arguing with John. If I encounter a problem where one of the partners appears to be extremely angry, it is far better to take them aside for individual therapy initially so that we can focus on why they are feeling this way.

One thing I should say here is that for all of us, the early examples of our parents' relationship, whether good or bad, will have a profound impact on how we, as adults, approach our own partnerships and marriages.

I offered John individual therapy as well.

'No thanks,' he said. 'Look, I think I am going to see what comes out of your sessions with Alice, then I'll be happy to go on with the couples therapy.'

'OK John, that sounds good. Although I would have preferred you to also have a few individual sessions. To give you the private space to express how you feel without any interruptions or disruptive outbursts.'

He looked at me thoughtfully and said, 'Although that is a good idea, I really don't feel at the moment that I need individual sessions.'

'OK,' I said, 'I'll carry on seeing Alice on her own for now.'

* * *

The first individual meeting with Alice was aimed at trying to get to the bottom of how she felt about the accusations she was facing from John. To all intents and purposes Alice looked like a very capable person. But I had the sense that, underneath all that, a frightened and vulnerable child was trying to make her voice heard.

When I said this to Alice, she was taken aback by what I had observed and confirmed that this was what she was feeling. I started to help her look back at her childhood and to recall her experiences growing up. I felt that the insight I needed was buried in her unconscious. It is widely thought that the unconscious is the part of us that will produce dysfunction.

A psychodynamic model is used to gain insight by:

- Getting in touch with the client's unconscious
- Bringing that which lies in the unconscious, into the conscious.

Although approaches that focus on feelings usually work towards insight, in the psychodynamic approach it is considered essential. You achieve insight when you understand what is causing a conflict. The premise is that if insight is gained, conflicts will cease. Achieving that insight can bring awareness, understanding and clarity to even the most complex situations. It can elicit the light bulb moments and may feel like coming out of a thick fog into the light, even a eureka moment.

In our first individual session, Alice opened up. Looking at her hands she said.

'I had been very depressed over the months before the condoms were discovered in the bedroom. I even felt suicidal.'

'Go on,' I said gently.

Alice spoke softly. 'I was sexually abused when I was young. It was a man who lived near us and he picked me up when I was walking home. He said he would give me a lift. Although I always had some memories of how I was abused it was not until recently when I moved closer to my parents' home again that I recognised how big an impact my past was having on my life.'

'You're doing very well, Alice,' I reassured her.

Alice cleared her throat. 'The biggest impact of that early abuse is on my relationship with John because I constantly feel that I'm going to lose him.'

'Have you told John about the abuse?' I asked.

'No I haven't but I have told him about my flashbacks,' she said quietly.

'OK Alice, we are going to need to work through the details of the abuse to process your trauma. Doing this will gradually lessen the intensity of those memories. You will be able to adopt new skills for managing any symptoms and you'll also be able to develop new patterns that you will be able to use within the relationships you have with other people.'

Alice was looking at me intently.

'The way forward', I told her, 'will include the positive outcome that will come when what happened to you has less of an impact on your life, but at the same time you will', I predicted, 'probably have difficulty when it comes to coping with any session where we focus on the details of the abuse.'

* * *

The mind blocks to protect. What I mean by this is that sometimes when individuals experience trauma like sexual abuse part of one's personality has been 'splintered' or 'broken' away. This part hidden by the mind is a form of protective amnesia usually to prevent complete shutdown of that individual. We need to think of our minds in the same way as a filing cabinet that stores memories, images, feelings and associations.

When we start to face the symptoms of trauma in therapy our 'filing cabinet' often will reveal hidden and suppressed files not remembered. This is a normal part of the therapeutic process of healing. However, a lot of clients when they are faced with this abrupt re-experiencing of traumatic memories feel they are getting worse rather than better. It is crippling I know and can consume one's life. The first thing though to remember is the memory is a past experience, no longer lived today.

It is always helpful to remind clients that to get better you have to ride the wave that comes home. Preparation and understanding are really important but there is life, light and hope on what is likely to be the long road to healing.

Over the first three sessions Alice was able to give me some description of the flashbacks she was experiencing. The flashbacks usually involved her being in a car when between the age of nine and ten, and feeling trapped. She couldn't see the face of the driver but he was exposing himself and trying to make her touch his penis. Alice went on to tell me that following the abuse she had started to sleepwalk and would have sleep terrors and nightmares. These things gradually disappeared in her late teens until recently, when over a few years she had begun to experience sleepwalking and night terrors again. I asked if she had any ability to recall her recent sleepwalking behaviour.

Alice said, 'Although I don't remember sleepwalking, I do have the evidence that I have done it. For instance, one morning when John and I woke up we found that bread had been toasted and was still in the toaster, cold and stale. On another occasion we got up to find the front door wide open although I know we had locked it before we went to bed the night before.'

I told Alice that I was confident that her sleepwalking had been triggered by her childhood experiences, and in particular by the sexual abuse. However, this needed to be explored further.

* * *

Sleepwalking occurs when we are in our deepest sleep and it is common in young children because they experience more sleep than adults do. We sleep most deeply in the first part of the night and it's most common that sleepwalking will occur at this time. In 2012, a groundbreaking study published in the American medical journal *Archives of Neurology* found that around 30 per cent of participants had a history of sleepwalking at some point in their lifetime (a figure far higher than previously thought), which suggests nearly a third of us have or could experience the phenomenon.

Contrary to what many people believe, sleepwalking does not always literally mean walking around while you're asleep. Activities that are also counted as sleepwalking can be things like appearing awake when you're asleep or sitting up while you're asleep. Some of the more common things that people do while they're sleepwalking may be to dress and undress, move the furniture around, even prepare a meal. Sleepwalking is generally not dangerous unless, in adulthood, the sleepwalker puts themselves or other people at risk of harm.

Although the reason behind it is not clear, sleepwalking and talking in your sleep may often be familial, although no specific genetic link has been identified. It is certainly true that there will be triggers for sleepwalking and these may include sleep deprivation, being stressed or anxious, having an infection, the recreational use of drugs or alcohol, and taking certain medications.

Sometimes being woken suddenly by a noise or the need to use the bathroom can trigger sleepwalking. People who suffer from restless leg syndrome also have a slightly increased tendency to sleepwalk, as do those suffering from sleep disordered breathing complaints such as sleep apnoea which causes them to wake suddenly from a deep sleep. Reflux and epilepsy have also been associated with a slightly greater tendency to sleepwalk.

There is however one sleep disorder that you may not have heard of and that is 'sleep sex' or 'sexsomnia'.

I thought of this sleep disorder as Alice described some of her sleep-walking patterns. 'Once John found me naked, walking on my own at night and realised I was sleepwalking,' she told me.

'Really!' I exclaimed. 'Has that happened more than once? Are there any other out of the ordinary behaviours you can tell me about that hap-pened while you were sleepwalking?'

'Well, yes,' said Alice. 'John has told me that on many occasions when I sleepwalk I tend to want to have sex with him, but I don't remember any of that the next day.'

This made me even more certain that Alice was probably suffering from sexsomnia.

I have never come across this condition before with a client and I needed guidance on what I should do. Unfortunately, the books I read were too theoretical and too generalised. None of the reading gave me any clear practical advice by suggesting how someone who suffers from sexsomnia might be helped specifically by a practical therapeutic approach. Fortunately, I found a colleague who was researching sleep disorders and who guided me along the way with any 'difficulties' I expe-rienced with this case.

Like sleepwalking, sexsomnia occurs while we are asleep but is related directly to sexual behaviour such as sexual intercourse and masturbation.

Alice told me that on both occasions when the condoms had been found in her and John's bedroom, they had found the front door open when they got up in the morning. I began to think there must be a connection between these facts, and my suspicion that Alice might be suffering from sexsomnia in some form became stronger.

* * *

During our next one-to-one session I explained to Alice about sexsomnia or sleep sex and what its effects would be on someone who had this condition.

I said, 'An individual who is experiencing sexsomnia or sleep sex may appear to be awake with their eyes open but what is really happening is they are experiencing an episode of amnesia and will be unable to recall anything about what has happened. Room-mates, parents or partners will often be the first people to notice what is going on. The person who is actually experiencing the sexsomnia or sleep sex will usually be the last to know.'

In fact this condition is a bit of a mystery, with no real figures as to how common it is, but in terms of psychological phenomena it is considered rare. Indeed, I had never come across anyone suffering from this condition in my practice so Alice was my first experience of someone with these symptoms. As a female, research indicates that Alice would be less likely than a male to have an experience of sleep sex or sexsomnia. However, it is also known that people with a previous history of sleepwalking, as Alice had, are more likely to suffer from sexsomnia.

I went on to tell Alice that it was important she realised that sexsomnia did not mean the person experiencing it was having sexual dreams; they were simply acting on autopilot. In fact there is the condition where a person may have sex without wanting to or even remembering that they have.

Not a lot of people, even medical and mental health professionals, know much about this phenomenon and it was only added to the *Diagnostic and Statistical Manual of Mental Disorders* (*DSM*) in 2013. The *DSM-5*[12] identifies sexsomnia as a 'specialized' form of sleepwalking under the classification of non-rapid-eye-movement (NREM)

---

[12] American Psychiatric Association (2013). *Diagnostic and Statistical Manual of Mental Disorders*. 5th edition. Washington, DC: APA Publishing.

sleep-arousal disorders and defines it as: 'varying degrees of sexual activity (e.g. masturbation, fondling, groping, sexual intercourse) occurring as complex behaviors arising from sleep without conscious awareness'. Minimal dream imagery is recalled, and amnesia for the episode is present. However, establishing the diagnosis of sexsomnia can be difficult, as various sexual activities during sleep have been described in different contexts.

Toronto Western Hospital, in 2013, did a study in which they found that 11 per cent of the male patients in the centre experienced sexsomnia compared to only 4 per cent of female patients.

There is some argument to say that the number of sufferers of sexsomnia is probably a lot larger than we know because those who suffer from it may be too embarrassed to seek help or may even be unaware of what is going on. However, the mental and physical toll on those people who do suffer from this disorder can be very damaging. It can end relationships, as the erratic behaviour of a sufferer is not understood. The sufferers themselves may be frustrated or feel embarrassed and guilty and it's even possible that there could be legal action if the sexsomnia leads the sufferer to attempt to have sex with a stranger. Now I wondered if this is what was happening to Alice.

At this point, we decided that it would be good for Alice to resume the joint sessions with John. There, they could talk about what Alice and I had discussed and see if we could find the reason for her sleepwalking.

When we met for the next session, I started by explaining to John about sexsomnia. I told John that in all likelihood the sleepwalking would occur in the first two hours after Alice had fallen asleep. Anyone who's ever had an experience with a sleepwalker will know that they appear to be in a very strange state and it is not usually very clear whether they are asleep or awake.

I also debunked the myth that a sleepwalker will be seen walking with their arms held straight in front of them, their eyes glazed and zombie-like, as is the popular depiction of sleepwalking. It is true, however, that sleepwalkers may have vacant-looking eyes and it will invariably be very difficult to get them to respond. When people sleepwalk they will rarely switch lights on to help them navigate around the house, as they would if they were awake. John asked me what he should do if he found Alice sleepwalking.

'To begin with, John,' I said, 'Alice will be so deeply asleep that she probably won't even notice you're there, even if you do make an attempt to wake her up. If you do manage to wake her up then you run the risk of making her very disoriented and even very distressed.'

'I see,' John said, 'but how am I going to know if she is having sex with someone else?'

And there it was, my dilemma. How would it be possible to discover if Alice was having sex with anyone while she was sleepwalking? I told John that if he did notice Alice sleepwalking and actually leaving the property, he could follow her at a distance to find out where she was going. I was not, however, 100 per cent in favour of this course of action because Alice could be put at risk if John did follow her.

I suggested they talk together and make the decision together. They both agreed that they would try to find out what Alice was doing when she was sleepwalking. John promised her if he thought she was in any danger he would gently guide her back to bed.

* * *

I would say that many clients I've seen over the years who have suffered some sort of sleep disturbance will have suffered a traumatic experience in the past. People often question me as to how something of this nature that happened often a very long time ago could have an effect on their present-day sleep patterns.

To answer this question, we should first understand what trauma is. In fact it's defined as anything that causes major damage to a person and is likely to lead to negative after-effects. Trauma is usually separated into two categories: physical and psychological.

Physical trauma would be any injury that causes bodily harm and quite often the term trauma is used to describe severe injury that can lead to a secondary condition, such as shock or death.

Psychological trauma on the other hand is any damage to mental health after an upsetting emotional or distressing event, such as rape or sexual abuse. In many cases psychological and physical trauma will happen at the same time. Clients like Alice who have been dealing with traumatic psychological issues, brought on in her case by sexual abuse, are quite likely to have sleep disorders and other syndromes, such as delayed phase sleep disorder, insomnia, obstructive sleep apnoea or, as in the case of Alice, sleepwalking.

Alice and John were due to return for another session after having a break of four weeks to monitor Alice's sleep pattern. It is important to mention at this juncture that often, when people go for therapy, they can experience a change almost from the beginning of that therapy, or may experience no change for weeks or months.

We may talk about the same things over and over again, going round in circles, before something happens: an insight, an understanding, a gush of emotions, a relief from tension. When and how we get to this point in the therapy is usually not predictable. We make small steps. There is often not so much an explosion but a natural process in how a client changes. I was therefore not sure what to expect in this follow-up session but was eager to find out if there had been any new revelations or observations about Alice's nocturnal behaviour.

In the nearly four weeks since I had last seen John and Alice, I had spent time researching sleeping disorders, especially sexsomnia, and had held lengthy conversations with my supervisor. I found out that during sleepwalking and sleep terrors, the part of the brain that generates very complex behaviours is awake, while the part of the brain that normally monitors what we do and lays down memories of what we have done, is asleep. This condition leaves the brain in a mixed wake/sleep state, capable of generating wild behaviours without conscious awareness and, therefore, without culpability.

It is not known what causes this 'state dissociation' (a mixture of wakefulness and sleep). I remembered from my psychodynamic course at Oxford that we have at least two streams of perception. One is of the physical world, the events we can see with our eyes or hear with our ears, for example. The other is the mental world, the subjective experience of our feelings, thoughts, hopes and dreams. And it was this world in particular that I was eager to discover in Alice's psyche.

* * *

On a Monday morning, my much-anticipated couple were eagerly waiting for me at the clinic in London. I cracked open the door to the waiting room and could see Alice and John sitting side by side. John was reading his book, dressed in a button-down collar shirt, penny loafers and corduroy trousers. Alice was sitting next to him, staring into space. She seemed tense and was leaning forward slightly. She was dressed in a brown, full-length coat clutching her bag.

'Why don't we step into my office?' I said to them both.

They followed me in.

It was John who answered my question as to how things had gone in their four-week absence.

'You were right,' he said, his face showing the strain he was under, 'Alice was sleepwalking and I followed her on several occasions. Every time I followed her she went to the same place, an area near her parents' home, where she grew up, which is also quite close to an area where prostitutes hang out in the town. You have to walk through that area to get to the estate her parents live on.'

This led me to wonder if Alice's sleepwalking was a way of re-visiting the place where she slept as a child or was traumatised as a child. It was a likely scenario but more pressing at this point was John's obvious deep unhappiness.

'Did anything happen on these nights when you followed Alice?' I asked gently.

'No, because I did what you said and turned her around and led her gently back home before she got too far into the red-light district. I was afraid for her safety.'

I nodded.

'The thing is, though,' John said falteringly, 'there are a lot of other times when I didn't follow her because I didn't notice she had got up. I have no idea what happened on those occasions, but with it being a red-light district, I suppose you wouldn't get any prizes for guessing.' He tailed off and I saw Alice look at him anxiously.

They had given me a lot to think about. She was in an area where, from her earlier description, was the place her abuser had picked her up in his car. Had she been sleeping with 'punters' on her nocturnal visits to the red-light district? The only thing I knew for sure at this point was that there were still far more questions than answers with this complex case.

We needed to find a way forward. Unfortunately, there is no specific treatment for sleepwalking or sexsomnia. In many cases simply improving sleep hygiene may eliminate the problem.

'Would you be happy to go, if I referred you to a sleep clinic?' I asked Alice.

She shrugged but I could tell that even although she was despondent, she would be willing to give it a try.

'I think that would be a very good idea,' John said. 'Can we continue to come and see you?'

'Yes, I think that you should,' I said, 'and I think it would also be a very good idea for Alice to see a psychiatrist who will be able to prescribe some medication.'

This roused Alice to ask why it was that her mind and body were reacting in such a way to her past trauma. I explained, 'Confusion, anxiety, physical arousal, and difficulty communicating emotions are common reactions to trauma. Some people, like you, experience a delayed reaction after traumatic events. These may include depression, fatigue, nightmares and, in some cases, sleep disorders. If these symptoms persist over time, or if they start to interfere with work or relationships, it is a signal of more severe post-traumatic stress.'

'And why do I need to be referred to a sleep clinic?' asked Alice.

'An assessment in a sleep clinic, Alice, is sometimes needed to fully understand and treat sleep problems such as yours. Most sleep clinics have purpose-built facilities for monitoring sleep which measure the pattern and depth of sleep and closely monitor breathing during sleep. So, when I refer you to a sleep clinic, Alice, you may be also asked to spend the night in a sleep lab so that your sleep can be monitored. Is that OK?'

Alice nodded.

John and Alice were happy to go along with my suggestions and Alice is currently under continuous observation to make sure she is safe while she is asleep.

This is a very interesting ongoing case and I am looking forward to seeing how Alice responds to medication and to the findings and suggestions of the sleep clinic.

FIVE

David

It's 7:00am on a Sunday morning, and I've been at home self-isolating for more than ninety days. I've lost track of time. I had to double-check on my phone calendar today to make sure it was Sunday morning. Now the government has announced more relaxing of Covid-19 restrictions. There's a feeling in the air as though people are coming out of a daze or a long sleep.

Quarantine has given all of us a lot of time on our hands, right? For me, being a psychotherapist and a researcher usually means spending hours seeing clients face to face at my clinic in London and also attending research meetings at my university to discuss and exchange ideas with my colleagues and friends.

However, the lockdown has taken its toll on all that. The coronavirus pandemic has resulted in many changes to our lives in the last few months, leaving many of us facing a variety of emotions. Whether it be growing fears over contracting coronavirus itself, cabin fever from being stuck at home day in day out, or a feeling of paranoia from self-isolating, everyone will have been affected in one way or another.

The lockdown has forced many of us to change our routines and plans, ultimately knocking our minds into an unfamiliar frequency.

The pandemic presents an exhausting list of unanswered questions: Will I be safe? Will my family be safe? How will we recover economically? And perhaps the most destabilising of all questions, how long will this last? The external world changes on a daily basis, which means that some of our normal coping mechanisms aren't functioning as well as they used to and we don't know what we need to do.

Having worked remotely for almost three months now I make sure that I treat my online sessions as if they are 'real' physical sessions and I am just meeting my clients remotely rather than in person. After all this is still *real life* therapy. It is face to face. It is not a poor substitute.

However, I did not always have the same opinion about remote sessions. When it comes to psychotherapy, I considered myself a traditionalist and was of the opinion that face-to-face sessions should always be held weekly, in the therapist's consulting room, sitting in the same chairs, and last for the therapeutic hour. Prior to the Covid-19 pandemic my view was that self-help, telephone, email or video sessions were inferior to face-to-face sessions between client and therapist.

However, since being forced to conduct psychological therapy remotely I have found that, much to my surprise, it works! My observations of what my clients experience matches the feedback that I receive from them. It is overwhelmingly positive. The coronavirus pandemic has brought questions of how we work to the forefront, not least the consideration of how therapy is delivered.

Fortunately psychotherapy and counselling can take place online just as easily as meeting in a room. I am sure if he were alive today, even Sigmund Freud would be sharing ideas with colleagues using email, Skype and WhatsApp as well as texting and calling on his mobile. Documents would be shared using 'cloud' services and university collaborations would be enabled via Zoom.

I think that Freud would almost certainly have been meeting some of his clients online and conducting therapy sessions remotely. However, to my surprise, having thought that online therapy is a recent development in mental health, I find that its roots go all the way back to the beginning of the internet revolution. The first instances of the internet being used was a simulated psychotherapy session between computers at Stanford and UCLA universities during the International Conference on Computer Communication in October 1972. Since then there is ample research that demonstrates that therapies such as cognitive behavioural therapy (CBT) are just as effective delivered over the phone or through remote online means as they are in person.

* * *

On this particular Sunday morning I received an email from a client who first came to see me approximately ten years ago. When David came to see me at my London clinic he was acting as a director for a retail company. Those who knew him, he explained to me at the time, would most likely describe him as a quiet, hardworking director.

I remember him saying that the daily hassles of working life, tight schedules, frustrations and high goals were sources of stress and offered the real threat of burnout for him. His daily activities included a punishing schedule of meeting clients, making presentations, travelling, as well as making critical decisions involving the company. These daily stressors and the increasing responsibilities of his role had led David to suffer from psychological distress and job burnout. Human Resources referred him to me and they were funding his treatment.

David successfully completed his burnout treatment and returned to work. He was not in a relationship at the time and dedicated his energy to building his career. He was living with his mother. His father had died when David was twelve, from a heart attack.

Before he died, David's father was an eminent doctor, a self-made man who overcame a deprived childhood to achieve an extraordinary reputation as a pioneering surgeon. His mother was a former school-teacher with a history of alcohol addiction and sexual abuse in her family. We never explored this aspect further when he came to see me as we focused on his work-related burnout and he also felt at the time that he was 'not ready' to talk about his childhood.

His email asked if I was able to see him again as he wasn't coping well. He explained that he had lost his job due to the pandemic and that his mother had died earlier in the year. He was now living alone in his mother's house. As I was the one who had treated him successfully previously, he felt comfortable talking to me again. We arranged a remote appointment for the following week to assess his current psychotherapeutic need.

I was mindful, however, that as a client who had been used to being in face-to-face therapy, he would have impressions and expectations of what therapy was like. It was going to be important to assess how these impressions and expectations might be influencing David's attitudes to starting online therapy with me.

* * *

As a rule of thumb, risky behaviours—such as suicidal tendencies or more severe psychiatric conditions like clinical depression and psychosis—are not always appropriate for online work. The reason for this is that as psychotherapists we occasionally encounter situations in therapy where clients are at risk of suicide, of committing a crime or suffering a worsening of their symptoms. These clients need to be handled in a way that is not possible in an online session.

If a client in online therapy suddenly becomes suicidal and hangs up during a session, no further assessment or risk reduction is possible. And it will be difficult to prevent that person harming themselves or other people. If they are in my office and they're suicidal, I can make sure that the client doesn't leave until they are safe.

The development of a safety plan from the start is needed to reduce the risk of crises and prevent adverse events. Instead, an appropriate response to emotional crisis is vital during online psychotherapy. The safety plan should include careful screening for risk of harm to the client or others before psychotherapy starts. We need to be on the lookout for any worsening of symptoms, and have a safety protocol in place that can mitigate for any crisis that occurs during treatment.

When a crisis like a suicide attempt does happen it is best to encourage clients to seek immediate treatment locally (e.g. for suicide prevention, medication assessment). Referral or assistance in finding an appropriate general practitioner or another appropriate source should be provided.

It all comes down to our personal preferences and specific circumstances, and some clients who are dealing with severe mental illness will respond more positively to intimate environments with face-to-face therapy while others who perhaps don't have a lot of time or find it difficult to come to the office will find weekly online therapy sessions a great and safe way to start the process of healing.

Ultimately though, whether a client attends online or face-to-face for treatment it is about one thing—a word that is repeatedly used in psychotherapy practice—'healing'. The concept of healing in psychotherapy is unlike the conventional understanding of 'healing' diseases, where the aim is to eradicate the disease.

In psychotherapy, mental and emotional issues are not to be judged as bad or to be removed; rather, these issues have to be understood. Depression, anxiety, PTSD and personality disorders aren't 'diseases to be cured'. They are opportunities for personal growth.

Furthermore, healing is not about reaching a specific point in time or any one goal. There is no such thing as the finish line where healing is concerned, although often clients come in desperate to be 'cured' of their emotional pain.

Unfortunately, our society is so focused on finding fast fixes to our problems that we lose the ability to sit with our pain and fully understand the root cause of our emotions. We have been trained to look for solutions that are fast, easy and effortless. Yet, in therapy, healing might take the form of embracing both the positive and the negative aspects.

To me, healing represents a journey in which you are able to explore the past and present and develop the tools needed to work through life's obstacles. As the great Stoic, Marcus Aurelius, wrote:

> Our actions may be impeded, but there can be no impeding our intentions or dispositions, because we can accommodate and adapt. The mind adapts and converts to its own purposes the obstacle to our acting. The impediment to action advances action. What stands in the way becomes the way.[13]

I am quoting the Stoic philosopher Marcus Aurelius because, like most therapists, I am surprised at how relevant Stoic ideas and other philosophical concepts are in psychotherapeutic practice. For example, the Stoics, like Plato, saw a clear distinction between 'illness' of the body and of the mind. The Stoic underpinnings can be clearly seen in the

---

[13] Holiday, R. (2014). *The Obstacle Is the Way: The Ancient Art of Turning Adversity to Advantage*. London: Profile.

therapeutic approach of cognitive behavioural therapy in the notion that individuals are not emotionally disturbed so much by events as by their negative belief about them.[14]

* * *

David and I had scheduled our first appointment on a Tuesday morning. I remember a few minutes before our remote session I was reflecting that, like most therapists, I've always kept a physical distance from my clients—other than the occasional handshake, or hand on the shoulder after an especially intense session. But being in the same room, hearing each other breathe, watching the tears flow or the sound of someone shifting in their seat, creates its own intimate closeness.

Although by now I had conducted several months of remote therapy sessions with clients and received encouraging positive feedback from the sessions, it was still a new experience for me with the same question in my mind: what would it mean, emotionally, for my client, when we were not in the same room?

When a client first comes to therapy, a space is provided. It is a space of time, an appointment time, a beginning and end time, a time to heal, usually an hour or so. There is also a physical space in the consulting room: two chairs, one for the client and one for me, with space in-between. That space between the two chairs allows for me and my client to be comfortable in a social and emotional sense. We like our personal space, so the distance between the two chairs is expected and feels somewhat 'natural'. But I believe also that space is more than physical and social, it can also represent an emotional, physical and spiritual value of a different sort.

The space between two chairs is also an area where self-realisation can occur. The space can be a place where our clients can ask or even demand, maybe for the first time, that they be taken seriously. This space can also be an important buffer between two people. The client may need a secure distance from another he may see as an authority figure.

I had to keep in mind the overwhelmingly positive feedback from other clients, and the more subtle positive changes that online

---

[14] Robertson, D. J. (2010). *The Philosophy of Cognitive-Behavioural Therapy (CBT): Stoic Philosophy as Rational and Cognitive Psychotherapy*. London: Karnac.

therapy had given rise to. I reminded myself that even clients like David, who in the past had been habitually late to sessions, due to the stress of driving or finding parking, could now be in the 'waiting room' early. However, there are many other reasons why someone might find it difficult to attend a face-to-face appointment: social anxiety, chronic illness, physical disability, difficulty taking time off work, difficulty finding childcare, living far from the therapist, and so on.

However, I have found that I do miss those first few minutes of a session that often are just someone taking off a coat, a handshake or settling into their seat in my office and exchanging pleasantries. These first moments allow me time to assess the more subtle unconscious messages of my client's 'state' of mind. Also missing was one of the fundamental props of any therapist's office—the box of tissues!

The tissue box on the table gives the client permission to cry, and tells them that weeping is allowed, even encouraged, in therapy. We place tissues with intention, so that they're visible and within our client's reach. Tears are serious business in therapy. When a client reaches out for the tissues it is usually a sign of relief, insight and change.

I don't take that lightly because as therapists we need all the information we can to help us understand what is happening and what needs to be done with our client's emotional state of mind. Furthermore, as therapists we look at the little things because sometimes they point to bigger things, and all that information can help us understand and ideally help our client.

I am reminded of Conan Doyle's Holmes in *A Scandal in Bohemia*, when Holmes instructs Watson on the difference between seeing and observing. He explains to Watson that to observe is above all to be conscious of what is in front of us, to be attentive when looking at the world. Holmes was taking note of the myriad inputs from his surroundings and was always observing and in touch with his environment. He had perfected mindfulness down to an art!

* * *

It was time to have my session with David. I waited to connect with him via Zoom. I had just taken my dog for a walk and loaded up the dishwasher, both activities that were very new and strange to me before a session in a working day.

The session began with David describing the depression he was currently experiencing after being made redundant during the pandemic. This was on top of the grief he had been experiencing since his mother's death. During the initial meeting, David spoke quietly and constantly broke eye contact, looking around him, while he spoke.

I said, 'What kind of thoughts go through your mind when you are having these sad feelings, David?'

'Well,' David said, 'I guess I'm thinking what's the point of all this? My life is over. It's just not the same. I think, "What am I going to do? I've lost my job and my mother."'

I said, 'I am so sorry, David. You've suffered such a terrible loss. No wonder you have been feeling so bad and having such a difficult time. It sounds like you are feeling quite bad right now. Is that right?'

David: 'Yes, I just feel that everything is completely pointless. I feel exhausted but I can't sleep. I feel hungry but I can't eat. My job was a killer but I miss it. You tell me, what is the point?'

David was really struggling to look me in the eye. I said, 'But you will get another job, David, surely?'

'I don't know. I don't really care. I don't care about anything.'

David was looking down at his hands and I could see that he was close to tears.

'How long ago did you lose your mother?' I asked him.

He flashed me a tortured look.

'Three months,' he said in a strangled voice.

'So not long at all. How old was she?'

'She was seventy-five.'

'Had she been ill beforehand?'

'Yes, she had been a drinker all her life and it finally caught up with her.' David shrugged, and dabbed his eyes with a crumpled tissue.

'How long had you lived with her?'

A flash of his eyes again.

'I've always lived with her. I've seen it all, all my life. I've even been in the middle of it!'

I heard a note of despair and something else in David's voice. Was it disgust?

'What do you mean, "in the middle of it", David?'

'Oh, she used to get me to drink with her, even when I was young, after dad died.'

David hesitated, as though he was about to say something, but had changed his mind.

'Things must have been very tough after your father died,' I said.

David nodded and seemed to be trying to fight back tears.

He was quiet for a time and I did not prompt him. I could tell that he needed time to collect himself and his thoughts. Eventually, still with his eyes averted he said, 'I had to take over my father's role when he died. Mum relied on me for everything: it was really tough on me, trying to live up to her expectations and the standards my father had set.'

He was silent again. I could tell that he was wrestling with something that he wanted to say, but for some reason was struggling with.

'What kind of things did you need to do, David?'

David shrugged again.

'Well, with mum drunk a lot of the time, and even more after dad died, I more or less had to do everything: the cleaning, the shopping and the cooking. I had to make sure that she paid the bills so that we did not have our electricity cut off. Sometimes she even used to call me by my father's name, as if she thought I was him.'

Again I had the feeling that there was something that David was not saying. He was now making eye contact with me a little more and I thought that it would be a good place to stop the session. We made a date for a few days' time.

* * *

On his next visit, David seemed to have more purpose about him. He looked me in the eyes when I greeted him and he seemed to have a set to his jaw that made me feel that he might be ready to talk to me and get to what was really behind his misery.

He started by saying that he was sending out applications for jobs.

'That's great, David,' I said.

'Yes, I think I might get an interview or two.'

'Well, I hope you do. How have you been coping with the death of your mother?'

David shrugged and looked down at his hands.

'I have been a bit better. Life was not always easy with her, you know.'

'Yes, you told me that she used to drink,' I said.

'She did, and she used to do more too,' David said and I felt that we might be getting to the heart of something now.

'What else did she used to do, David?'

'She sexually abused me when I was young, when dad died.' David gave a sharp intake of breath as he finished his sentence as though he was afraid of what my response would be.

During the remainder of our session David's sentences fluctuated between slow soft speech and impulsive spluttering outbursts and I could see he was fighting back tears. It has been almost ten years since David last tried to speak to me about his childhood memories and I guessed he had spent much of his life trying to suppress his mother's abuse.

The experience of sharing such a trauma, for the first time, must have been a gruelling undertaking. He had clearly been feeling trapped by his past all these years. Being able to finally talk about his abuse must have been a great relief for him.

'I see, that must have been very traumatic for you,' I said gently.

David nodded and then suddenly put his head in his hands and started to sob.

At this point I realised that I needed David to achieve resilience in order to help him to mobilise his own capacity for self-repair. He needed the ability to tolerate negative feelings and to be able to use self-regulatory strategies when he was distressed.

What I mean by this is that I would help David to identify and interpret his emotions and put them into words. The question many will ask is why, after all this time—almost ten years—had David finally disclosed his abuse over the span of only three sessions? It is important to bear in mind that just because a client comes to therapy it does not always mean that they are ready to change. David attended for therapy ten years ago and was ready to look at his work-related burnout issues but did not have the 'readiness' to look at his unconscious traumatic events.

* * *

Therapy is a deeply personal and often a very challenging process. Many clients have to go through different stages within the process of therapy before they can create a deeper understanding of their own psychological and emotional issues. Entering therapy involves an honesty and open-ness to be able to address the personal and emotional challenges we face every day, and these are often challenges we choose to hide from our conscious minds.

It requires developing a trust in a therapist to embark on self-disclosure and the client needs to welcome the therapist into their often emotionally fragile world. It often pushes us to challenge our self-perceptions—and the perceptions of those around us—and assess the thought patterns and coping habits that have become second nature. Most clients will go through different stages of readiness.

The 'Transtheoretical Model' (also called the 'Stages-of-Change Model'), developed by James Prochaska and Carlo DiClemente in the 1980s,[15] is a good description of the different stages of change clients can go through.

The initial stage is usually called the **pre-contemplation stage**. This refers to the stage in which there is still a resistance to change and this can also be referred to as the 'denial stage'. A useful distinction can be made between a problem that is admitted to by a client and an attributed psy-chological issue that others have noticed the client displays. While family and friends may comment on a client's psychological symptom, individu-als at this stage may well be unaware or unconscious of their problems or may be unwilling or discouraged when it comes to changing them.

If pre-contemplators present for treatment, they often do so because of pressure from others; for example, a spouse threatens to leave or par-ents threaten to disown them. The next change of readiness we see in our clients is that of the contemplation stage.

Individuals in the **contemplative stage** are willing to consider the possibility that they have a problem, and that admitting this offers hope for change. However, I have also noticed that clients who are

---

[15] The following are two good chapters on the subject. Prochaska, J. O., Redding, C. A., & Evers, K. (2002). The transtheoretical model and stages of change. In: K. Glanz, B. K. Rimer, & F. M. Lewis (Eds.), *Health Behavior and Health Education: Theory, Research, and Practice* (3rd edn.). San Francisco, CA: Jossey-Bass. Prochaska, J. O., & DiClemente, C. C. (2005). The transtheoretical approach. In: J. C. Norcross & M. R. Goldfried (Eds.). *Handbook of Psychotherapy Integration*. Oxford Series in Clinical Psychology (2nd edn.) (pp. 147–171). Oxford: Oxford University Press.

contemplating change are often highly ambivalent in our sessions. They are on the fence.

Contemplation does not mean commitment. It is important to remember that it can be hard to give up the known—no matter how distressing and painful—and to travel to an unknown place that will require change and risk.

The stage of readiness that follows the contemplation phase is that of the **preparation stage**. This is considered the information-gathering and planning process of therapy. However, being prepared for action does not mean that all ambivalences within a client's psychological state of mind have been resolved. The challenge at this stage is to help clients develop a change plan that is acceptable and effective.

I usually accomplish this by helping clients identify any existing motivating factors and use these elements to get them to embrace more motivating factors.

Motivated and committed to treatment is the stage that most psychotherapists are working to help their clients reach. It is what we call the action stage, and that was David's current stage of readiness. A client in this phase has actually begun doing some things differently, and may be experimenting with expanding their efforts.

In the **maintenance stage** people will have sustained their behaviour change for a while (more than six months) and have the intention of maintaining the behaviour change going forward. People in this stage will be motivated to work to prevent a relapse to any of the earlier stages.

This is obviously not a 'perfect' model but it does help to put clients' efforts into perspective and to cajole them towards the right direction.

Survivors sometimes cope with abuse by attempting to 'put it behind them' and are unaware of a connection of their current life difficulties to their childhood trauma.

David's disclosure of his trauma in our session would have given him a type of vindication and that would have allowed him to let go of a lot of the horrors and tortures of having been sexually abused. Recovery from the abuse is non-linear and it is impossible to predict the length of time each person will need to make progress at any given stage.

* * *

In David's next session I said to him: 'David, you have taken the first step to recovery from abuse by bolstering your inner strength with a tiny bit of hope and a drop of self-love. What was once a painful memory will become a liberating factor of your truth. The shame will slowly disappear and will be part of your testimony. Now is your time to heal and grow.'

David replied with a shake of his head: 'I have never told anyone my secret until now, in our sessions. I was too embarrassed to tell you this when I saw you ten years ago. I felt it was not something to share because it was so painful. In my heart, I always wanted to tell someone. But I thought—who would understand me and would I be judged?'

At this point our session came to an end and David rebooked his remote consultation for the following week. After I wished David goodbye I sat by my desk to reflect on the day's therapy.

I stared out of the window into the garden and noticed my favourite maple tree next to the pond. I was gazing at the green arrowhead leaves floating on the water when suddenly a few of the goldfish leaped up as if escaping from an enemy below and dropped back again making overlapping circles ripple across the water. I pondered on how our thoughts are like the fish, hidden and deep underwater, and, like the fish, surface only briefly when fear triggers them to.

I often use the sea as a metaphor to explain the overwhelming feelings of trauma to clients, comparing trauma to the vast depth and spread of the ocean. I ask clients to imagine that they are stuck and abandoned in the middle of the sea all alone after a shipwreck. Then I ask what they think they would do next?

Usually, my clients will say that they should fight and swim as hard as they can back to the shore. But, I will say, sooner or later you will only end up exhausting yourself and you will not get closer to safety. When you are exhausted, I point out, you are at higher risk of drowning. In fact, experts advise the best thing you can do in this type of situation is to allow your body to relax, and conserve energy by allowing yourself to float, instead of fighting the waves. This gives you a better chance of getting through the ordeal and allows time to calm yourself so you can think clearly about what to do to survive.

When my clients experience the symptoms of trauma I advise them to do the same thing; to relax and allow themselves to 'float' or 'ride' the waves instead of fighting the symptoms. Unfortunately, resisting and avoiding these symptoms as David has done for most of his life often brings on more intense emotions like frustration, anger and ultimately depression.

* * *

As a society we have finally begun to face some important facts about sexual abuse. The dissemination of new information and a change in social attitudes towards sexual abuse has helped some survivors to remember the abuse that has long been repressed. It has helped them to find the inner strength to share their trauma with someone.

Over the years I have seen a number of clients—men and women— who as children or young adults endured sexual abuse at the hands of their mothers or other female carers. Very few of them had ever had a chance to express their abuse and kept their experiences to themselves.

I also remember, over the years, a few clients telling me that they did try to disclose what was happening to them to family members or to their doctors but they were met with a similar dismissive and disbelieving response: 'Mothers don't sexually abuse children!' So the question is, why such resistance and reluctance to acknowledge the truth? Why is there such a denial of female sexual abuse? Paedophile predators come in all shapes and sizes, male and female.

There are enduring myths that surround our ideas of paedophilia— including ideas about the type of people who abuse children.

There is a widespread misconception that all child sex offenders are men. This benefits female abusers because there is a reluctance to accept or believe that sexual abuse of children can occur at the hands of women. There are some significant distinctions between male and female child sex abusers. Females, on average, offend against younger victims and are less discriminatory in terms of victim gender. There are several hypotheses as to why women sexually abuse children.

According to research, some women abuse their daughters due to narcissistic tendencies. In these cases, an older woman's need for admiration, combined with an exaggerated sense of self-importance, leads her to be jealous of her own daughter.

A significant number of females who sexually abuse children fall into the 'teacher/lover group'. This group comprises women in their thirties who victimise males with an average age of twelve years. The women may see the relationship as being based on love, and may not see it as abusive or recognise it as inappropriate. They can be driven by a need for intimacy and may be trying to compensate for emotional needs that are not being met elsewhere.

This group can include the female teacher who becomes sexually involved with a male pupil. They are invested in the idea of a relationship and find adolescent boys less threatening than men of their own age. They may feel that they have more control over a relationship with a young boy.

Another category is one that researchers have termed the 'predisposed molester'. Women in this group have often experienced abuse themselves and may have addictive personalities. A similar category, of the 'mother molester', may comprise a significant proportion of female child sex offenders.

Research has routinely indicated that women are 4.5 times more likely to offend against their biological child, as well as other children in their care, than against strangers. One thing is for certain: sexual abuse can profoundly interfere with normal developmental processes that occur in every subsequent developmental phase of a person's life, from the time of the abuse throughout childhood, adolescence and adulthood. Treating adult survivors and addressing the painful memories of childhood and the accompanying affect is essential for the resolution of sexual abuse.

* * *

We had booked our tenth remote session and I remember that in this particular session, we sat in what seemed to have been a moment of silence as the pain of recollecting his mother's abuse proved too intense for David.

Clients who have experienced sexual abuse often cannot clearly describe what has been done to them. Some clients describe sexual abuse trauma as being like a snake residing in their mind that moves quickly and slithers away before you can get a good look at it. This is why we also refer to sexual abuse as hidden, analogous to invisible toxins in a glass of water: you cannot see or feel the 'poison' until your body and mind starts reacting to prolonged exposure to these toxins. In therapy, we refer to this type of shame as 'toxic shame'.

This is also the shame that David brought into the therapy session. The shame born of experiencing psychological and physical trauma that creates emotional paralysis and its prolonged isolation results in the interruption of our emotional, personal and professional development. Sexual abuse is as shameful and toxic as it is because the person who should feel the shame of it—the abuser—usually never owns it and a victim like David ends up carrying the shame.

And this is exactly the way abusers work, in a hidden and sneaky way that exists under the radar. They disguise themselves. But what happens if the abuser is a family member, someone you trust, like a mother? Unfortunately, female/mother sex offenders have rarely been studied and are poorly understood.

In our society mothers are not viewed as violent or aggressive but rather gentle and passive and are expected to rear children with warmth and love. So when this primary protector becomes abusive to her child it becomes a challenge to the image of motherhood in the psyche of our society, almost always leading to secrecy.

As in David's case, most mother–child sexual abuse survivors report that this is the most hidden part of their life and that the secrecy perpetuates the toxic shame of childhood. The shame that keeps the abused child and later on the adult shrouded in secrecy and a world of isolation goes unnoticed and is not easily identified.

* * *

This kind of dysfunctional behaviour pattern between mother and son is referred to as overidentification. The *Oxford Living Dictionary* defines it as, 'The action of identifying oneself to an excessive degree with someone or something else, especially to the detriment of one's individuality or objectivity'.

However, I favour the notion of enmeshment developed by psychotherapist Salvador Minuchin to characterise family systems with weak, poorly defined boundaries. It is a form of inappropriate bonding, a 'blurring' of parent–child boundaries often practised by mothers on their sons in the absence of a father. The mother emotionally and psychologically elevates her son to a 'husband' and 'friend' status by filling the void of loneliness she is experiencing.

I am by no means undermining a healthy mother–child bonding. I'm referring to the situations when there is a lack of these healthy boundaries that should exist to safeguard the relationship between parent and child. In the absence of these safeguards the child is brought up in an environment that is unpredictable, chaotic and emotionally and physically unsafe.

* * *

At our next session David asked if, now that he had disclosed his mother's abuse, he would need any further sessions.

'You don't *have* to do anything, but it will certainly help, David,' I said. 'Imagine if you completed your first year at university, then skipped on to your final year and took your final year exams. What do you think will happen?'

'I would probably fail,' David said.

'Exactly! Recovery just doesn't *happen*. It evolves by learning one thing after another in a gradual process. There's no magic to it, but there are building blocks to recovery, David,' I said.

'That's helpful, Stelios.' David looked thoughtful. 'So how can I start understanding, for example, the symptoms of my depression? Because sometimes I feel like I am going out of my mind!'

That was an interesting remark David made: 'I am going out of my mind.' I have heard this countless times over the years from clients.

But when we say, 'I'm going out of my mind', where exactly are we going? Research suggests that the 'mind' isn't confined to our brains, or even our bodies.

Dan Siegel, a professor of psychiatry at UCLA School of Medicine and the author of the 2016 book, *Mind: A Journey to the Heart of Being Human*,[16] defines the mind as 'the emergent self-organizing process, both embodied and relational, that regulates energy and information

---

[16] Siegel, D. J. (2016). *Mind: A Journey to the Heart of Being Human.* New York: W. W. Norton.

flow within and among us'. He suggests that our minds contain our perception of our experiences as well as the actual experiences themselves. Professor Siegel explains that 'the mind is a complex system' and, as such, 'optimal self-organization is: flexible, adaptive, coherent, energized and stable'. Considering this description as the 'foundation to mental health', he says that without the 'self-organization part, you arrive at either chaos or rigidity'.

* * *

In this session and throughout our therapy relationship, David recalled and reiterated the devastation he experienced from his mother's abuse.

Answering David's questions concerning his symptoms of depression, I said to him: 'One way that you can understand these symptoms is to look at them as a way of your body and mind communicating a message. So if you are feeling depressed this is a message that something in your current life needs to change. It is similar to the pain you experience when your burn your fingers. When you feel the burn you react quickly as the signal from the pain helps you react and a protective mechanism kicks in to prevent further injury occurring.

'In the same way, when we are overwhelmed by traumatic memories and feelings we ask ourselves how these can be examined and changed. What I mean is that therapy will give you the opportunity to see your present situation from another point of view. What may initially seem to be emotionally overwhelming will appear very different after a few weeks or months of therapy. Your ability to change your perspective will help you tap into resources which you may not even be aware you have, which could also help to resolve your own predicament.'

'So how do I do that?' David asked.

'Well, David, perhaps it will help to answer your question if you first understand the three Ps of pessimism, developed by a therapist called Martin Seligman in his book *Learned Optimism*.[17] He suggests that clients who are going through a depressive period have a way of thinking that is habitual and that they may view themselves

---

[17] Seligman, M. E. P. (1991). *Learned Optimism: How to Change Your Mind and Your Life*. London: Nicholas Brealey, 2018.

as **p**ervasive, **p**ermanent and **p**ersonal. For example, when you have a flashback of your mother abusing you and the feelings become unbearable, you might say to yourself, "I'm always going to feel like this" (permanent), "I will never be able to stop these feelings" (pervasive), "It's my fault that my mother abused me, I am an evil person" (personal). This way of examining your thoughts is part of a cognitive approach to your depression.'

David looked up from where he had been gazing down at his hands.

'Are we using a different type of therapy now then?'

I smiled. 'As I explained before, David, I am an integrative therapist, and integrative therapy is a form of psychotherapy that integrates different therapeutic techniques and approaches to best fit the needs of a client. It's a more flexible and inclusive approach to treatment than the more traditional, singular forms of psychotherapy. Does that make sense?'

David shrugged his shoulders slightly. 'Oh, yes it makes some sense but how many approaches are there?'

'Well, as integrative therapists we combine two or more theories in different ways, to understand and to assist a client with their current psychological needs. However, one of the most important steps in therapy is helping clients to become empowered. Once a client realises they are empowered, they are then free to generate changes that will produce a healing outcome and a secure control of their future. Does this explanation help you, David?'

David nodded and I continued. 'In my opinion an integrative model allows me to find ways to fill the gaps that I find exist in some theoretical models. I have never adhered religiously to any particular given "school" as I find all, in some ways, can have their limitations when it comes to addressing the range of needs for my clients. As a therapist, I always think we should be guided by a sense of wisdom in our practice because not all life and therapy can be catered for by one recipe.'

'I see.' David was looking interested.

'What I mean is that the wisdom is to be able to relate to our clients. It is going to be very difficult, as a therapist, to help our clients if we don't apply wisdom and compassion to what we do.'

'So you have to learn too!' David gave a small smile, the first I had seen from him.

'Yes!' I smiled back. 'We can cultivate wisdom within ourselves by practising mindfulness-based therapy. When you look into your inner life during meditation you develop a sense of wisdom about how your mind works and you will also get a better idea of your own personal strengths and limitations.'

'I've heard that,' David said.

It turned out that this wisdom would be much needed for what was going to develop with David's therapy.

As therapists, sometimes when we encounter a client who is resistant to change, the temptation is to label them as 'difficult' largely due to our own frustrations. This label is unhelpful as it creates a distance between the therapist and the client and makes the therapeutic connection even harder, although in David's case it was quite hard to avoid the fact that he was proving difficult to help.

David had another appointment the next week but he cancelled it. Then he cancelled the one the week after and did not make another. It was a month later that he got back in touch. As we sat looking at each other on our screens he was visibly thinner and was again unable to meet my eye.

'How have you been, David?' I asked.

'Not good.'

'Oh? What has been happening?' I enquired.

He sighed and looked down at his hands. He took a couple of breaths in as though he was about to speak but each time exhaled without saying anything. Finally, on the third attempt he blurted out: 'I tried to end it. I tried to kill myself by drinking a bottle of vodka and taking two packs of paracetamol.'

He was mumbling and rushing his words so much that I barely understood him. But I had got the gist of it.

'Well, I am very sorry to hear that, David. But I am pleased that you called for help before it was too late. That is a very positive thing.'

'I don't feel positive. I feel as though I should be dead.'

'And yet you did not go through with it?'

'No. I suppose I'm just a coward,' he said, and I could tell he was close to tears.

'Or you realised that you can get through this.'

David shrugged.

'Well, I have some good news, David. Now that the Covid-19 restrictions have eased a bit we can meet again, face to face at the clinic in London.'

'Oh?' David looked up and I saw his shoulders come up out of their slump a bit.

* * *

Unfortunately, attempted suicide is not uncommon for survivors of sexual abuse. Children who have experienced abuse will develop different biological and emotional pathways to other children who have not been brought up with abusive experiences such as sexual abuse. It is true that any one of us can experience emotional trauma during our life but the devastating consequences of trauma during infancy and childhood are much more severe and long lasting.

This is due to the fact that as children our early relationships with our caregivers are commonly known as 'attachment' relationships and have an enormous impact on our developmental and emotional brain. Furthermore, early attachments with our caregivers are the foundations on which we build conscious and unconscious psychological models in regard to our interaction with the world and how we see ourselves in that world.

It is these unconscious psychological models that I'm trying to help David bring to the surface of his conscious mind so that he can challenge and rectify them.

However, one of the most devastating and catastrophic results of abuse is that these unconscious models become ingrained within our perceptions, our minds, making it difficult for us to segregate the traumatic experience and the impact it has had in our lives. This results as an error in our self-perception in the form of a thinking distortion that suggests our suffering is a consequence of 'who we are'.

Exploring David's unconscious world and the wounds that reside there will help him ultimately find new and healthier ways to relate and cope with them. This does not mean that as part of David's healing process his past traumas will no longer affect his life—after all, we cannot change our past experiences or replace them like an old car part with a new one—it is more about reducing the impact of childhood trauma by creating a more meaningful and spiritual life.

Clearly, David coming to the therapy sessions physically was going to be the best way forward for him, especially in view of his recent suicide attempt. I was also pleased to know that he was under the supervision of a colleague of mine, a psychiatrist, and was on medication, which I was confident would help as we continued on the long road to David's recovery.

SIX

Abigail

W hat happens when you start holding onto decades of worthless bank statements, newspapers, old clothes, expired food and other seemingly useless items? When your corridors are beginning to be stacked floor to ceiling with papers, old furniture, and other defunct items? Perhaps you find yourself having to pick your way through a 'tunnel' or a 'goat trail' to get through the maze of things piled up as you go from room to room of your house. And once you have managed to crawl through, possibly injuring yourself in the process of reaching your bedroom, you find your bed stacked high with clothes and shoes with no spare inch for you to get into it?

Maybe you try to get into your bathroom but find the entrance completely blocked by stacks of used toiled paper and the floor littered with faeces from your fifty cats? Not to mention the bodies of decomposing pets littering your home and outnumbering the living ones!

Recognise any of this? Or the potential to end up like this? You have hoarding disorder—a mental health condition characterised by a compulsive need to acquire and keep possessions, even when they're not needed or are even repulsive (such as faeces, rubbish and dead pets).

You could be forgiven for thinking that hoarding is a very modern phenomenon, and it is true to say that from the twentieth century this kind of behaviour has increased and evolved in dramatic fashion.

Although social factors play a part, recently academic analysis has focused on psychological features, not really accounting for the changes to this condition over time or the effects on those who suffer from it. Scott Herring's *The Hoarders: Material Deviance in Modern American Culture*[18] provides us with a great resource from which we can trace the trajectory of hoarding both as a behaviour and as a disorder.

* * *

In the year 1937, the appearance of the word 'hoarding' dramatically increased in frequency in scientific publications. This was observed against a background, in the USA, of the Great Depression. At that time George Ford Smith wrote, 'The Great Depression brought hoarding and inflation to centre stage,' demonstrating a direct correlation between deprivation and the tendency to hoard. Under these circumstances, hoarding meant exercising personal control over an increasingly over-whelming economic situation, and trying to adhere to an older and more stable financial system.

From a personal and domestic point of view, hoarding in those days was referred to by a variety of names in the decades before its formal designation as a disorder, including synonyms like Collyer Brothers syndrome, chronic disorganisation, pack rat syndrome, messy house syndrome, pathological collecting, clutter addiction, etc.

A modern demonstration of this tendency has been seen in more recent times with the infamous hoarding of toilet rolls in the UK at the beginning of the coronavirus pandemic. When people feel threatened with being unable to get what they need, the instinct to hoard will kick in. However, in most people, once they feel that the threat of deprivation has passed, they will go back to their old habits of collecting what they need, when they need it. This is where the roads of normal behaviour and hoarding, or compulsive behaviour, part company.

------

[18] Herring, S. (2014). *The Hoarders: Material Deviance in Modern American Culture.* Chicago, IL: University of Chicago Press.

Hoarding occurs when a person psychologically and physically cannot let go of material possessions, even when they may cause harm and obstruct living space. Hoarders' beliefs about their possessions are so powerful, it is difficult for them to eliminate the beliefs and the clutter. For many people, hoarding symbolises a more unconscious or hidden problem which is being 'acted out'.

The term 'acted out' was originally reserved for clients attending psychoanalytic therapy but now has become a common parlance for behaviours that are 'bad' or 'unhealthy'. For example a classic 'acting out' behaviour is observed in young children engaging in temper tantrums at a supermarket or your pet dog barking incessantly. However, in psychodynamic therapy it is an expression of repressed emotions surfacing in the conscious behaviour of our everyday lives. So, for example, when we are deprived by a partner of affection and love, we may 'act out' by compulsively shopping, which makes us feel better. Or, when we are stuck in a job we hate but don't have the courage to leave, we act out and exhibit inappropriate behaviours at work that get us into trouble and ultimately cause us to lose our job so we are forced to find another one.

We all 'act out' to some degree and in various situations; this is not reserved for those who attend therapy. Yet the most common outcome is that we won't get what we want by acting out. There are other ways of achieving our goal, be it love, affection, another job or healing, by asserting ourselves or seeking the appropriate help. The biggest stumbling blocks will be the 'fears' that we experience, such as the fear of being humiliated or losing someone we love.

In therapy, acting out negative emotions can be contrasted with communicating them in ways that are more beneficial to the sufferer, such as by talking, art therapy, psychodrama or mindful knowledge of the feelings. Furthermore, during therapy, the development of a safe and constructive expression of conflict is an important part of personal development and self-care.

At the time of writing this chapter the *Daily Mirror* ran a piece entitled 'Britain's biggest hoarder!' The piece, written by Tom Davidson, told of how the hoarder was forced to move into a bed and breakfast for the last year of his life because he simply could not even move in his house any more. This hoarder apparently amassed a treasure trove worth as much as four million pounds that was made up of over 60,000 items, all contained within a terraced house in Nottingham.

The home of the man dubbed Britain's biggest hoarder was filled floor to ceiling with items he had been collecting over a lifetime. When authorities finally got into the property, they found that the majority of items consisted of parcels that had been delivered but not opened going back to 2002.

He had been forced to make contingency plans during his hoarding career as his need for space got greater, and he had apparently rented two garages, a section of a neighbour's garden, an additional one-bedroom flat, and twenty-four wheelie bins to accommodate his massive collection. The clean-up operation took the council 180 hours over a six-week period as eight men worked with three vans to remove bags and boxes and other rubbish from the house. Even to get into the house they had to work by clearing a path for themselves, removing boxes one after another so that they could get into the interior.

Once the items had been removed, they were put up for sale in an auction house where a further eighteen people were needed to unwrap all the unopened packages. Three rooms of the sale house were devoted to storing the 3,000 lots that would eventually sell over four days. Estimates for the likely price of the hoard ranged from between half a million to four million pounds. Many of the items for sale were brand new and had never been unpacked by the owner of the house, a man in his forties who died suddenly. He had worked as a computer programmer and where he got the money from to amass his huge collection was not known.

* * *

Compulsive hoarding, in my experience, is a way to communicate feelings such as abandonment, loss, rage, fear, grief and shame. People who are compulsive hoarders often speak of an emptiness or void inside. When I visit a hoarder's house, as I do on the documentary series *The Hoarder Next Door*, broadcast on Channel 4 between 2012 and 2014, I am constantly astounded by how clutter is often displaced in a dramatic and symbolic fashion (making no sense to others, sometimes not even to the hoarder themselves).

These visits always remind me of the pharaohs of Egypt who on their last journey (death) would have their important possessions taken into the pyramid or underground chamber to be placed inside their tomb so that they could have them all with them in the afterlife.

We become attached to people and things because they serve a perceived need, which we think if we can just attain, will somehow complete us. Attachments are tricky. Our freedom goes out of the window, and we react emotionally. When we hold onto things, we are doing that based on hope. We hope to lose weight, catch up on reading, finish that abandoned project, and a hundred more hopes. It is similar to the good intentions of the New Year's resolution. And we all know where most of them end up by the middle of January! The problem is that when we fail to realise our hopes or resolutions, it's hard not to feel guilty about it.

Attachment and loss are inseparable—to become attached is to suffer the possibility of loss. One thing is certain: each one of us will experience loss. Significant loss often heralds a time of deep sadness, emotional pain, and perhaps even a sense of hopelessness or despair. It can be an inconsolable time.

* * *

My first encounter of hoarding behaviour was back in the early 1990s, early in my career as a psychotherapist; in fact, I was not yet out of training. I got my first therapy placement in an NHS eating disorder unit. I remember sitting for days in a redecorated broom-closet-cum-therapy-room being a consistent 'object' available at the same time and in the same place for my clients every week.

To understand what I mean by being a 'consistent object' for my clients, we need to understand the psychodynamic concept of object constancy which originated from the concept of object permanency (a cognitive skill we acquire at around two to three years old). It is the understanding that objects continue to exist even when they cannot be seen or sensed in some way. In adulthood, object constancy allows us to trust that our bond with those close to us remains intact even when they are not physically present, picking up the phone, responding to our texts, or even becoming frustrated with us. Absence, in the context of object constancy, does not imply disappearance or abandonment, but rather a temporary separation.

For example, borderline personality traits are characterised by a lack of object constancy. For those who are insecurely attached, any distance, even if it is brief and insignificant, causes them to relive the agony of being abandoned, dismissed or treated with contempt. Their fear may cause them to engage in coping survival behaviours such as denial, clinging, avoidance and dismissing others, as well as lashing out in relationships or a pattern of sabotaging relationships to avoid potential rejection.

Without object constancy, people are more likely to be viewed as 'parts' rather than 'whole'. They struggle in the same way that a child struggles to understand his or her mother as a whole person who sometimes rewards and sometimes frustrates them. Relationships may appear untrustworthy, vulnerable and overly dependent on the mood of the moment to them. There appears to be no consistency in how they perceive their partner—it shifts from moment to moment and is either good or bad.

Working with eating disorder clients made me realise how lack of food or the experience of starvation can be a difficult situation for any individual to deal with. The most common hoarding behaviour, I noticed at the time, was that of hoarding food. When you don't eat enough food, your brain perceives that food is scarce. When your brain perceives that food is scarce, it may also come to the conclusion that essential resources are scarce. Hence, the desire to hoard all sorts of items after a prolonged energy deficit.

My first ever client back in that broom closet was a young lady who suffered from bulimarexia. This particular eating disorder is a combination of anorexic and bulimic symptoms. The patterns of perpetual symptoms include prolonged periods of fasting whilst using laxatives followed by a binging and purging cycle where the bulimarexic client consumes a vast amount of food and then vomits sometimes as much as twenty or thirty times a day. The consequence of such 'abuse' to the body results in organ damage, damage to the enamel of the teeth, and reduction of bone mass.

The symptoms of hoarding food with eating disorder clients is often not the only symptom and can be accompanied by other symptoms such as:

- Stealing or hiding food
- Eating rapidly over a short period of time

- Storing or stashing food
- Becoming emotional if food is limited, taken away or if forced to share with others.

The two disorders of anorexia and bulimia in bulimarexia have common tendencies which include:

- Indecisiveness
- Anxiety
- Depression
- Social factors/dysfunction
- Genetic/hereditary links.

I see now, after twenty-five years of working as a therapist, that it is quite possible that many of the clients I treated for eating disorder were also likely to be hoarders. Hoarding behaviour and eating disorders are also closely associated with obsessive compulsive disorder (OCD). Unfortunately these days the term 'OCD' is often used flippantly and jokingly. But OCD isn't anything to joke about. This often misunderstood mental illness is characterised by thoughts and behaviours that can make it extremely difficult for people to go about their daily lives. That is because OCD involves repeated and sometimes intrusive unwanted thoughts or urges that cause a person various degrees of anxiety. To reduce the anxiety they feel, the individual will perform compulsive actions or rituals.

Someone with obsessive thoughts centred upon safety might lock and unlock their front door or a car door dozens of times before they feel they can leave the house or drive away. Other patterns might be persistent thoughts around an obsession with dirt or germs or constant doubts about being the cause of an accident.

The compulsions and obsessions that are associated with OCD will sometimes result in someone having real difficulty getting rid of or acquiring items or possessions. For example, OCD sufferers may fear that something awful will happen if they throw something away. Others may feel incomplete when something is given or thrown away and might even want to document and preserve things that remind them of specific times in their life. They might, for instance, keep all the childhood toys they had.

In some cases, a fear of contamination might lead to reluctance to throw things away or get new things. With fears that anything on the floor could be contaminated, an OCD sufferer's floors become covered with items that should have been thrown away. Someone exhibiting contamination fears might buy everything in a shop that they had touched—and 'contaminated'—to stop others being contaminated.

'Magic numbers' is another recognised pattern of behaviour that leads to excessive acquiring of items. Here a person feels they need to buy everything in multiples of a 'magic number'.

A person may avoid throwing old post away because doing so would bring on endless, anxiety-ridden checking rituals. Sometimes a fear of making a wrong decision about getting rid of something may be so intense that it becomes easier to just never throw anything out.

The OCD hoarder will often be unable to part with things that simply are no longer needed, holding on to things in case they might be needed in the future.

In the past, hoarding was usually associated with OCD. The *Diagnostic and Statistical Manual of Mental Disorders, Fifth Edition* (DSM-5) now makes a distinction between forms of hoarding associated with the obsessions and compulsions of OCD (as described above) and a separate disorder: hoarding disorder.

One of the most difficult aspects of compulsive hoarding is that people who hoard may not recognise their behaviour as a source of risk to themselves or others and may refuse to engage with agencies that try to help them address it. They may, however, experience significant anxiety and shame as a result of how others react to their property. This can lead to increased isolation and may exacerbate the risk. Repairs and maintenance, for example, may not be completed if tradesmen are not contacted or are denied access. Similarly, friends, relatives and support agencies may be kept at a distance, exacerbating the hoarder's isolation.

There are many theories about the triggers for compulsive hoarding and how it should be treated. The causes will be complex and different for each individual and my experience indicates a combination of stresses experienced during childhood and other traumas may well be triggers. Furthermore, research now suggests a strong genetic predisposition. However, nothing prepared me for the complexity and intricacy of a recent referral of a client who suffered from compulsive hoarding.

* * *

Abigail was referred by a colleague of mine who was working as a prison psychiatrist (also referred to as forensic psychiatry and in the US as psychiatry for the court). Abigail was under psychiatric care after attempting to hang herself while in prison. It all started when Abigail's hoarding had got out of hand. Her difficulties with organisation and discarding her possessions had resulted in a cluttered environment in her home. As a result of her embarrassment about others seeing her home in this state, her main disability had been complete social isolation.

Abigail's hoarding issues began in childhood. She admitted in the psychiatric report to hiding things under her bed so they wouldn't get thrown away. She also remembered being a fearful and anxious child. Since childhood, Abigail's hoarding symptoms had waxed and waned.

Her report described how in some places in her house the clutter reached a height of four feet. No rooms in the house could be used for their intended purpose, especially the kitchen, which was completely unusable due to the accumulated clutter. Using trails to get around the house was only partially possible because tables, chairs, couches and floors were almost completely covered with items. Newspapers, magazines, bills, videos, clothing, bags of garbage, and books were among Abigail's hoarded possessions. Abigail's main hoarding concern was clothing from various charities.

The local council had been called in after complaints from her neighbours to clear the vermin-infested house she was living in. While the council workers were clearing her house, they found the skeletal remains of two newborn babies in her bedroom, 'completely intact' skeletons, dressed in dolls' clothes and shoes.

The infants were found buried in the corner of her bedroom under a mountain of garbage, as if a truck had dumped its load on top of them. It was later discovered that the two bodies buried in the hoard were twins. Furthermore, the referral report from my colleague included police photographic evidence of the hoard and the dead infants, providing me with a clear picture of the severity and enormity of the hoard and living conditions. The police report and forensic evidence indicated that the infants were stillborn. Abigail disclosed to my colleague that, 'The babies were my father's after he raped me.'

Abigail described how from the age of six her father had started sexually abusing her and continued to do so into her twenties, progressively worsening into torture and rape. It only ceased when he died from a heart attack. Reports from neighbours indicated that Abigail had moved in to her terrace house eight years ago when she was twenty years of age.

Her notes indicated that Abigail's mother suffered from mental health problems, such as compulsive hoarding, depression and severe anxiety that had started a few months after Abigail was born. Apparently Abigail's mother was admitted to a psychiatric ward twice after trying to take her own life and Abigail spent most of her early childhood with her maternal grandmother (who was also a compulsive hoarder) but with periods of time spent with her father.

Abigail recalled that her father was distant during her early years and did not support her or her mother. Her mother eventually succeeded with one of her suicide attempts while she was in a psychiatric ward when Abigail was six years old. After her mother's tragic death, Abigail continued to live mostly with her grandmother although she did also spend time with her father and his new partner.

Abigail appears to have struggled to cope with her mother's suicide and engaged in some self-harming behaviour that was recorded by social services, who were monitoring her from the age of twelve. The types of self-harming behaviour that she indulged in were activities such as superficial cutting and head banging.

It was at that time, approximately at the age of thirteen, she was admitted to her local child and adolescent psychiatric ward after she was found by her grandmother trying to strangle herself with a scarf in her bedroom. There is also a psychological report during her early admission suggesting that she was suffering from an altered state of consciousness, commonly known as dissociation.

Dissociation for traumatised individuals becomes the only way to exist and, as a result, the natural growth and development of a sense of self becomes fragmented because information is cut off. This information can include feelings and memories. When this happens the natural growth of our emotional development and our sense of self-awareness is also cut off or dissociated. Dissociation, therefore, represents a separation from those experiences including physical and emotional experiences, memories, perceptions and identity. Dissociation is a naturally occurring defence against childhood trauma and it is thought that children dissociate more frequently than adults.

If a child is suffering from extreme abuse it will often be observed that the child withdraws within themselves and psychologically flees from the experience that they are suffering from. This is the development by the child of a dissociated defence mechanism and if this continues into adulthood full dissociative disorders can develop. There are five dissociative disorders:

- Dissociative amnesia refers to the situation when a client is unable to recall important personal information especially regarding a specific event; they have literally blanked it out of their mind.
- Dissociative fugue. In this condition a client will find that they have arrived in a place but that they have no memory of getting there and sometimes have no knowledge of who they are.
- Depersonalisation disorder is, as described before, when a client is detached from themselves, their personal feelings or the situation they are experiencing.
- Dissociative identity disorder. In this condition, a client has two or more identities within the core of their own persona. This state has also been referred to as multiple personality disorder.
- Dissociative disorder not otherwise specified (DDNOS). We use this description when there is no obvious label for the symptoms that a client is exhibiting or when a full diagnosis has not yet been given to them. It is also important to bear in mind the common symptoms that cover these dissociative disorders. They are amnesia, depersonalisation, derealisation, identity confusion and identity alteration.

The psychologist who was treating her at the time noted that Abigail would describe these altered states as being outside her own body and being disconnected from others and her actions. It was also clearly documented that Abigail suffered incest from both her father and his new partner.

Sexually abused clients tend to engage symbolically in communicating their emotional and physical abuse. On many occasions the emotional and physical abuse is communicated through actions, words and metaphors they use, including sensations in their bodies and repetitive patterns in everyday living.

It is important to bear in mind that the abuse of a child and the psychological trauma they experience due to that abuse is an affliction on the powerless. The young person during the traumatic experience is rendered powerless and helpless against the overwhelming force of their abuser. Due to this overwhelming sense of helplessness and the limited coping capacity, a child has to defend him- or herself by dissociating. Dissociation enables a young person to temporarily or at least emotionally distance themselves from such traumatic experiences.

Sadly, Abigail was first admitted to hospital when she was sixteen after a serious suicide attempt and remained under close supervision in a local psychiatric ward for two months. The notes also described that although she was kept in the secure psychiatric ward, she still overdosed on a large quantity of saved-up medication and continued self-harming and mutilating her legs and stomach with a stolen metal fork.

However, the most destructive and painful aspect of trauma is the ingrained and habitual self-fulfilling cycle of the mistaken belief that our emotional suffering is the result of 'who we are'. If we believe that it is part of our character, we are likely to believe that there is nothing to be done about it. If we are shy or reserved, we think that will always be our fundamental way to be, and without any other point of reference it is easy for an abused person to think that is just their place or their lot in life.

The forensic police report noted that questioning of Abigail's neighbours revealed a consensus that she wasn't sociable, and that they had noticed she became more reclusive over time and much more unkempt and dirty. Eventually Abigail wouldn't speak to any of her neighbours and occasionally she was found drunk outside her front door. Her neighbours were also really surprised that the two infants' bodies were found in Abigail's house because she lived alone and they had no idea she had even been pregnant. Neighbours did say, though, that they were aware that, on occasion, family members would come and visit her.

What was the most amazing thing was that Abigail had now asked to see me and be referred for therapy because she remembered seeing me briefly some years earlier. I remembered the time. It was a period when I was working in a secure child and adolescent unit. At the time I was conducting group work with adolescents on the subject of self-harm and eating disorders in teens, and I assumed she was one of the young people in that group.

Unfortunately, I only remembered her vaguely as this was a psycho-educational group, not an individual one-to-one session. The group itself was for educational purposes so obviously you didn't get to know the individual in the same depth as you would in an individual therapy session. Nevertheless, I was eager to meet her again and understand the tragic circumstance that had led to her current condition and, of course, how she had ended up with two dead infants buried under a pile of rubbish in a rat-infested hovel of a home.

* * *

Now, apparently the time had come for her to be discharged from prison. One of the requirements of her discharge was that she engage with a mental health team and receive psychological support for her mental state and her hoarding compulsions.

It was at this point that Abigail asked specifically to see me as she worked towards her prison release in some twelve months' time.

It was late morning on a March day and due to the vagaries of the British weather there was a heavy snowfall to negotiate on my way to see Abigail.

As I arrived my first impression was that the prison walls seemed more as though they were protecting a castle rather than a prison. The building was wedged in a narrow corner of a congested suburb. I passed through a number of checkpoints before I entered the visitors building area. I was wondering if I would recognise Abigail. It had been so many years and I had a vague recollection but I really wasn't sure I would recognise her immediately.

I remember as I reported to the officer in charge at the visitors building that I thought how run-down and depressing the place was. The paint looked faded and the secretary had a look on her face that definitely said 'Don't mess with me' as she sat next to her rusty filing cabinet. A prison officer with a craggy face that spoke of many years of exacting service greeted me. He extended his hand and said, 'I've been expecting you. What's the weather like out there with all that snow?'

'It's pretty bad. Everything is at a gridlock, so I'm pretty concerned about how long it will take me to get back home,' I tell him.

He gave me a crooked smile. 'Well, I'd still rather be out there than working all day in here.'

We both smiled.

'OK, Mr Kiosses, just follow me this way please.' I was shown into what looked like an interrogation room and indicated a chair with a stained and gouged plastic seat.

'You have one hour to see Abigail. Just wait here and she will be brought along soon.'

In fact it was about an hour until a different prison officer entered the room. I had checked my watch at least a dozen times. I was concerned about the weather. From what I could see through a high small window, the snowfall was getting stronger.

The officer who eventually arrived was much smaller than the previous officer and moved very slowly and quietly. He apologised for the delay in Abigail being brought to see me but did not elaborate as to the cause. He asked if he could get me a drink and I said, 'Thank you, just a glass of water please.'

He disappeared, and as I waited I remember feeling a sense of oppression. Apart from distant noise it was very quiet, and I could almost hear my heart beating. The prison was having an effect on me, its walls seeming to close in on me. I sat, watching the snow coming down, and started thinking again about the journey home. The trip to see Abigail was obviously going to take a lot longer than I had anticipated. I would get home a lot later; that's if I managed to get home at all. The snow outside was almost a white-out now.

A genteel knock on the door preceded the return of the prison officer, this time followed in by Abigail. The young woman smiled at me as she walked into the room. The officer asked Abigail to sit down. She walked over to the other side of the desk and sat down on the plastic chair opposite me. 'I saw you looking out the window. It's snowing outside. Is it really bad?' she asked.

'Yes, it is pretty bad out there. Driving here was quite tricky and I don't expect it to be an easy drive home.' I smiled reassuringly. Abigail looked nervous and I could see beads of sweat on her forehead.

'It is nice to see you again, Abigail, especially since it is so long since we last met. I have read the file about you, that your psychiatrist sent me, and I do remember the last time we met, although I have to say, not very well.'

Abigail still looked very nervous despite my attempts to relax her with my preamble. I gave Abigail some more time to relax, and answered a few questions that she had for me before I moved on to an introduction in which we discussed what we would be doing in her therapy sessions.

'To begin with, Abigail,' I said, 'we are going to explore what traumas you experienced in your childhood and later on as an adult. We are going to explore how these traumatic experiences have affected your emotions, your relationships and how you behave. This should help you and it will also be the first step towards recovering from challenging experiences that life has dealt you.'

Abigail was looking perplexed. She raised her hand, as though she were in school.

'Is there something you don't understand?' I asked.

Abigail nodded. 'What is trauma?'

'Trauma can be a single event or a series of events that include things that have happened to you, like sexual and physical abuse that make you feel helpless and afraid.'

'Like what my father did when I was a child? That was a trauma?' Abigail asked.

'Yes, that's right, Abigail. A child can become traumatised if he or she is abused by an adult who is meant to be caring for them. The abuse usually makes them feel ashamed and embarrassed and they often think it is their own fault. But it is never the fault of the child!' I exclaimed.

'I see,' Abigail said. 'Is this going to help me with my hoarding too?'

I smiled. 'That is what we are aiming for, Abigail. It should also help you with your hoarding. I will be using a combination of therapies called cognitive behavioural therapy and psychodynamic therapy.'

Abigail: 'Wow, what are they?'

I said, 'Well, Abigail, the first type of therapy, called cognitive behavioural therapy or CBT for short, is about what you think the meanings are behind the experiences you've had in your life. As humans we constantly interpret what is going on around us and form beliefs and understandings of the experiences we encounter. These beliefs affect how we actually see the world. Sometimes our thoughts are distressing to us and can lead us to act in ways that are unhelpful. I am going to help you look at the beliefs you have and make sense of what they mean.'

Abigal was staring at me almost unblinkingly. She nodded.

'The other type of therapy I will be combining with CBT is psychodynamic therapy. This type of therapy will help you understand the patterns in your emotions, thoughts and beliefs to see why you do the things you do. These patterns are often found to have started in childhood, since psychodynamic theory says that early life experiences influence psychological development and how an adult functions. Psychodynamic therapy should help us identify important pieces of the puzzle that makes you, you; and then rearrange them in a way that will allow you to have a more functional and positive sense of who you are.'

Abigail gave me a bewildered little smile. 'OK, I don't know if I understand all of this but I do trust you.'

I smiled back. 'That's great, Abigail, but don't worry. I will explain all this again and again if it becomes confusing during our sessions. But tell me, Abigail, why did you decide to see me?'

After that Abigail started to talk. The first thing that I noticed about her voice was the audible pain and sorrow she was clearly feeling. She started off by explaining why she had specifically asked to see me.

'I have a few reasons that I asked to see you. I remembered you from the group therapy session you did back when I was sixteen and suffering from anorexia. Because of it being a group, I never had the chance to speak to you then. I wanted to but I was just too scared. I remember that you were there for three sessions and after every one of them, I tried to get up my courage and come and talk to you, but I guess back then I was a bit more shy.' She gave a self-deprecating little giggle that was born more out of embarrassment than mirth.

I smiled at her.

'Yes, I am sorry, Abigail. I was appointed by the child and adolescent unit for only three weeks to help you all as a group where, if you remember, we were talking about self-harm and eating disorders and there was no way to see anybody individually.'

She nodded and looked at me.

'The thing is ...' she said, looking down. The end of her sleeves were balled up in her fists. I noticed her nails were bitten down almost to the quick.

She glanced up at me again and said, 'It's really hard for me to open up to other people, even to friends and family, but I need to speak to someone so that they can hear me and just be with me without judging me. I just always thought you were that person.' She shrugged, 'But I never got the chance to do that until now, when I asked for you to come.'

She looked a bit surprised that her request had been granted. It was an important moment. Abigail had decided to trust me. What she said to me and where that went would not be possible without this early attachment.

'Go on,' I said gently.

Abigail looked down at her hands again.

'You know I was abused, right?'

'Yes, I do, Abigail, I've read your file.'

'And you know about the babies, right?'

I nodded.

'Thing is, my dad always fiddled with me, you know what I mean?'

'Yes, I understand,' I replied.

'It was horrible,' Abigail said, and her face contorted slightly before she gave another little shrug.

'I suppose you just get used to it in the end. Well, at least I did, and even when he started to rape me that probably wasn't so shocking because of all the stuff he'd done before. Anyway, with mum gone, he didn't even have to worry about her finding out, and things got a lot worse because the woman he was seeing joined in as well. I found that weird because I didn't think that women did that kind of thing.

'Dad belonged to a biker gang and the other men who were in his gang used to hang around our house all the time. I used to hide in my bedroom to keep away from them but one night Dad brought one of them into my room. I can remember the man saying, "She's a scrawny little thing, ain't she?"

'I remember dad laughing and pulling me up off my bed.

'"Beggars can't be choosers," he said, and I could see that the man was undoing his trousers.'

For a moment Abigail stopped talking and closed her eyes. I could see her eyeballs moving behind her eyelids and I was pretty sure that she was replaying that horrible night like an old movie.

Abigail cleared her throat and it sounded to me as though she was choking back tears. 'Well, he was the first one, but there were about another eight to come after him, nine if you include dad. I tried to keep my eyes shut all the time because I didn't want to see their faces. I could smell the booze on their breath and most of them stank of BO and piss. When it was over and they'd all left, I thought dad might come in to see if I was alright or to say something, but he didn't.'

Abigail stopped talking again and took a few deep breaths.

'It was probably about three or four months after that that I realised I was pregnant. I knew the baby was dad's, or one of his friends, and I knew that that wasn't right. So I didn't tell anyone and he didn't seem to notice. Then he had a heart attack and died. The woman he was with buggered off, never even said goodbye!'

Abigail gave a long shuddering sigh.

'Anyway, when the babies came, I was at home and I was really frightened, especially when I realised that there wasn't just one. They didn't look right when they were born and I realised that they were both dead. Funny thing is although I felt sorry for them, I was glad too because I didn't know what I would have done or how I would have looked after them. With them being girls as well, I thought they would be lucky to be dead rather than having to go through what I'd been through.'

Abigail's voice dropped.

'I dressed them up in some dolls' clothes I had. Of course, I was only expecting one baby but I had dolls' clothes for two, so I could dress them both up nicely, shoes and all! I thought about taking them outside somewhere to bury them, but we didn't have a garden and I didn't know where I would get a spade to dig up the ground anyway.'

It was a desperately sad story and I felt very sorry for Abigail. She was a very slight girl with mousy hair and a defeated air about her. She had been in prison for repeated shoplifting and because it had been determined that the babies were stillborn, she was not going to face any charges in connection to their death. I realised that it was going to be very difficult to get this young woman to overcome her severe trauma and her hoarding habits so that she was able to pursue something approaching a normal life.

* * *

Unfortunately, the abuse Abigail suffered is not unique and happens to women and men of all races, ages, cultures, religions, socio-economic levels, and sexual orientations. Sexual abuse trauma can be at the root of numerous psychological problems, including depression, anxieties, poor self-esteem, abusive behaviours, social problems, sexual and food problems, chemical or sexual addiction.

Unlike some of these conditions which can be hidden to some extent, for instance when someone is feeling depressed and still puts on a brave face and gives a false impression that they are coping, with compulsive hoarders they literally create a mess so visible and 'loud' (I call it visual noise) to others, that the disorder is extremely difficult, if not impossible, to disguise or hide. The difficulty is that compulsive hoarding happens behind closed doors, as we see in my TV show, and it can stay invisible to the outside world for a very long time—until some sort of crisis happens—as in Abigail's case, where she was sent to prison and the council was called in to clear her home.

The most common and stereotypical perception of hoarding is the 'cat lady' with dozens of cats in her home, or the idea that hoarders are messy, dirty and lead chaotic lives. In fact, there is no evidence to suggest that hoarders are necessarily dirty, messy or unhygienic. An even more surprising idea might be that children and young adults can be hoarders, but are often not seen as such because parents are in control of their environment and activities, or see low-level collecting as just a 'phase'.

My initial objective in seeing Abigail for the first time after so many years was to get her to come back again to see me and continue her therapeutic process when she left prison. Development in any therapeutic relationship is based on trust. However, trust can mean different things to different people. Although it is obvious that as a psychotherapist one must be trustworthy, in helping a client that is not as easy as one would think.

One aspect I have found to be the most important element in sustaining the establishment of trust is allowing clients the intrinsic right to be their own person.

At this point it is important to mention that the psychotherapy profession is unique in that it strives for two fundamental processes:

- Helping clients through normal life transitions not only during catastrophic and dysfunctional times
- Working with clients towards prevention.

Abigail's next appointment would be at my consulting room. She would return to her house, which had been decluttered by the council.

Treating a hoarding problem is far more complicated than simply cleaning the individual's house and throwing the accumulated possessions away. If the underlying issue is not properly treated, the hoarder will simply begin accumulating new possessions, quickly refilling the cleared space. Television and other popular media have brought hoarding into focus, hopefully sparking further research into the underlying causes of this behaviour.

This was also one of the main reasons that I agreed to be part of the television show, *The Hoarder Next Door*. The symptoms of hoarding can be seen on the programme as a kind of fortress that protects the individual and his feelings. Hoarding represents coping tools that are very hard to give up. In denial, the compulsive hoarder will often refuse treatment, so compulsive hoarding can be a serious illness that is very damaging to the mind, body and spirit.

We all live life in terms of our own story. As the emotional and physical clutter for a hoarder increases, it becomes more infused with their identity and so their 'preciousness' and overattachment towards the item increases. Hoarding syndrome is associated with older age, anxiety, limited adaptation, and poor insight into the disorder. It often accompanies social dysfunction, functional disability, impaired functional recovery, increased risk of mortality, severe psychopathology (e.g. anxiety and depression) and diminished quality of life.

Other characteristics include perfectionism, indecisiveness and procrastination. It is associated with OCD, obsessive-compulsive personality disorder (OCPD) and other psychological disorders (e.g. mood disorders, schizophrenia, dementia, eating disorders, mental retardation). Compulsive hoarding is now officially recognised as a disorder in the *Diagnostic and Statistical Manual-5* (2013).

Like many people, I collect various items (in my case, books). Collecting is a natural human activity and some evolutionary psychologists have argued that it may have had an evolutionary advantage in our past history (e.g. there may have been periods of severe deprivation where hoarding was adaptive and enhanced the probability of reproductive success and human survival). However, for a small minority, collecting and hoarding can become excessive and pathological.

* * *

Once Abigail was released from prison, she did come to see me at my consulting rooms. As she took her seat, she said, 'I haven't been collecting stuff, honest!'

The fact that this was her opening statement, made to me so vehemently, made me pretty sure that she was, indeed, hoarding again. I knew the council had cleared her property but now that she was back in it, clearly the problem was continuing.

I asked Abigail how she'd been and she shrugged.

'Alright, I suppose. It was a bit of an effort getting my benefits sorted but that's all right now.'

I asked her, 'Were your mum and dad on benefits when you were growing up?'

Abigail gave a hollow laugh.

'Probably, but whatever money they had, they spent on booze and fags mostly. And, of course, dad spent it on his bike or stuff for his bike. I can remember asking him if I could have an extra blanket because I was so cold in the winter that I couldn't sleep but of course I didn't get one.'

'How old were you when he started to abuse you, Abigail?' I asked gently.

'Dunno. Maybe about eight? Actually, it was when I asked for the extra blanket and he said he would be able to warm me up. At first, I thought it was a nice thing for him to do, until he started pushing his fat fingers into me, because that hurt.'

* * *

When survivors talk about sexual abuse, they may experience a wide range of emotions. They might feel the horror and pain of the abuse. Survivors may also feel guilty at what they believe they should have done differently. These powerful mixtures of emotions should not be discarded, but should instead be considered and examined.

Psychodynamic psychotherapy has been shown to be effective in treating clients with trauma as a result of sexual abuse. I therefore use some of these distinct features of psychodynamic psychotherapy as the focus of the treatment.

These features involve: discussion of past experiences, identification of recurring themes and patterns, and exploring attempts to avoid aspects of past and current experiences. 'Follow the red thread' is a phrase that encourages the therapist to concentrate on the thoughts and emotions that arise during the therapy session rather than being distracted by trivial problems and situations.

To do so, we must, as therapists, be empathic and nonjudgemental, listen to the client's discomfort and demonstrate empathy in order to provide a comfortable environment for talking with our clients.

However, having a strong understanding of clinical principles is advantageous. The methods used in dealing with sexually abused clients vary significantly from conventional therapeutic techniques. Students in psychotherapy that have no didactic and supervised clinical experience in the field of sexual violence and abuse will not be properly equipped to effectively advise sexually traumatised clients. Clinical trainees could find it difficult to develop therapeutic relationships and treatment plans and to keep the right professional boundaries with their clients without adequate training.

Studies show that therapists who counsel clients who have been sexually abused are at risk for experiencing vicarious traumatisation. Vicarious trauma is the emotional residue of exposure that therapists have from working with people as they are hearing their trauma stories and become witnesses to the pain, fear and terror that trauma survivors have endured. Vicarious trauma can impact a therapist's professional performance and function, as well as result in errors in judgement and mistakes. It is recommended, therefore, that mental health professionals should be educated further about sexual abuse, sexual abuse myths, PTSD as a result of sexual abuse, and about sexual abuse perpetrators.

* * *

'Can you remember when you first used to collect things?'

'It was when I was about ten maybe. It was a time when there was lots of litter on the street. One day I was walking down the path near the shops and I saw a ring pull from a can lying on the street. The sun was shining on it and it looked like something golden. I picked it up and that was probably the start of it. I gathered up any that I found and kept them in a carrier bag at home. I liked the way they sounded when I shook the carrier bag and if I put them on my windowsill when the sun was out, they shone really brightly. They made me feel like I had some real treasure and that one day I could buy a ticket to get far away from him.'

'And the abuse was continuing?' I asked.

'Oh yes, it was what you would call open season on me. He just raped me anytime he felt like it. He would try to make me go down on him, but I told him I would bite it off,' she sniggered. 'Then he would say he would knock all my teeth out if I did, but he never made me.'

'You told me the new woman he lived with joined in?'

'Yeah.' Abigail looked thoughtful. 'She did. Like I said, I didn't know then that ladies would do anything like that. They would like me to watch them at it as well and I found that really horrible. They both looked like fat pigs and they sounded like it too. I never got any peace from them abusing me, until he died.'

I realised after our first session that I would need to visit Abigail at her home to see what the situation was and how much she was hoarding. Home visits are not unusual for health professionals, especially if you are working within a community mental health team or if you are a community psychiatric nurse or psychological well-being practitioner.

Also, on occasions, psychological interventions can be more effective outside the boundaries of the consulting room, such as interventions in the treatment of phobias. For example, meeting clients who are agoraphobic in an open space or perhaps flying with a client who has a fear of flying as the final step in the therapeutic intervention. Or helping a client's complicated grief by accompanying them to the cemetery or to a funeral, if the client requests it and it is clear that he or she would not go on their own.

When visiting a hoarder's house, it provides me with an opportunity to become familiar with the individual's own hoarding turf. It enables me to observe the home with its clutter and get a first-hand sense of its organisation, hygiene, and any potential risks. Home visits to a hoarder's house reveal an enormous amount of information in comparison to a clinic-based therapy visit. This type of boundary crossings in therapy are well-constructed treatment plans that can increase therapeutic effectiveness.

We made an appointment for me to visit Abigail at her house. When I turned up my heart sank. One glance through the window told me that the situation was already pretty bad. It seemed even though the council had cleared her hoard she had lapsed back into her hoarding behaviours.

Abigail seemed excited to see me and led me through a corridor piled up with empty tin cans in carrier bags into her lounge, or what you could see of it under neatly parcelled-up packages of newspapers that lined the walls and had totally engulfed the settee. There was a strange muffled quality to the sound in that room as Abigail had unwittingly produced very effective soundproofing.

Two threadbare chairs with a rickety table between them occupied the space beside the window but I could tell from the indents on the cushion of my chair that it had probably, until just before I arrived, been a resting place for more of Abigail's accumulated clutter. Abigail had emptied the contents of a packet of rich tea biscuits onto a cracked plate and now offered me a cup of tea in a grimy-looking mug. I took it and sat down.

Treatment for hoarding disorder can be difficult because many people are unaware of the harmful effects of hoarding or do not believe they need treatment. This is particularly true if the items or animals provide solace. People often respond with rage and anger when their belongings or animals are taken away, and they quickly gather more to help them meet their emotional needs. So I was not that surprised to see Abigail's house full of clutter again.

It's also important, once again, to differentiate between clutter and hoarding. Hoarding is the accumulation of a large number of items, often of little value (e.g. ketchup packets, newspapers). Since it is excruciatingly difficult for a hoarder to let go of objects, they will not do so. As a result, things pile up in dangerous ways, they are frequently unable to find items, they don't clean because there is simply too much to clean or it is too difficult to clean, and they find their personal and professional relationships being affected.

Clutter, on the other hand, is essentially a messy environment; but, unlike hoarding, the home is safe to walk around in. Some people collect a lot of things, but unlike a hoarder's belongings, these items that clutter up the house have value or personal meaning. People who have a clutter problem, on the other hand, may have difficulty getting rid of the clutter and keeping their home tidy. They may discover that they are unable to decide which valuable item should be kept and which should be discarded. Even if they get help cleaning or organising, they may find it difficult to keep the place clean. Even if it is clean for a short period of time, the clutter usually returns.

Hoarders attach emotions to items. By letting them talk about why certain items are important to them, we can help them realise what the emotional attachment is in their memories, not the physical item itself. Therefore, my initial question concerning Abigail's hoard was pertinent.

"Why are these items important for you, Abigail?" I asked, indicating the contents of the room with a sweep of my arm.

Abigail looked embarrassed.

'I've been collecting newspapers. I never buy one myself, but I pick up ones I find in bins or, sometimes, I get new ones from the railway station if the bloke on the ticket desk isn't looking. The *Metro*, do you know that one? They give it free to people who travel on trains.'

'I do know the *Metro*,' I told her. 'But what do you collect them for?'

'I like to read the stories in them,' she gave a wry chuckle, 'to see if any other buggers have had it worse than me!'

'Do you read them all?' I asked.

'Nah, I'm not that quick at reading, that's why I keep them all!' she said; her voice held a note of hope, that maybe I would see this as a reasonable explanation for what she was doing.

'And the tin cans?'

Abigail bit her lip. 'Well, I think they are just nice to have. So many different colours, and types. And then there are the ring pulls. I've liked them since I was a little girl. They are my treasure.'

Abigail hoarded many different items, including clothing, books, figurines, furniture, kitchenware and paperwork. In describing her hoard, she recounted personal and emotional memories of people or events that different items would bring up for her. She also reported that she shopped when she felt lonely or empty. She informed me that some items seemed to bring on strong emotions like anxiety and other negative feelings. When I asked what those items were she pointed out some of her old clothing like a red skirt she had worn when she was a child around the time she was being abused by her father.

As an exercise, I asked her to collect a few emotional items for our next session as I wanted to explore her memories and feelings concerning her traumatic abuse but also wanted to broach a subject we had not yet spoken about fully: the birth of her twins.

* * *

On her next appointment at my consulting rooms, as I watched her walk up the street outside, it struck me how young she looked. Although I knew that she was twenty-eight, she could pass for half that.

Abigail seemed pleased to be in the consulting room again.

'Is that the couch what I'm supposed to lie down on?' she giggled.

'You can if you like, but the chair will be fine too,' I said.

She sat on the chair and stroked the arm of it as she looked at me expectantly. 'Nice chair!'

'Thank you, Abigail. Shall we talk a bit about your past?'

'S'pose we better,' said Abigail, shrugging her shoulders.

'OK. So when did you realise you were pregnant?'

Abigail shook her head.

'My periods were always up the spout, so it wasn't unusual to miss some, so it was probably about three to four months. Funny thing was that I didn't really feel different at all. Until the last night.'

Abigail raised her hand to her mouth and chewed on a painfully short and red-raw nail.

'I had my own house that I moved into when I was twenty but it didn't stop that pig coming around to rape me whenever he felt like it.'

Abigail frowned deeply.

'Anyway, the night it happened I had kind of a tummy ache so I went to bed early and I must have gone to sleep. I felt like I was in a bad dream, that I had a lot of pain and then later on I fully woke up and I thought I'd wet the bed but when I got up and put the light on, I saw it was blood, lots and lots of blood and in the middle of it were these two little babies. They were really tiny and they looked a bit like aliens to be honest with you. Anyway, I was absolutely petrified.'

Abigail chewed hard on her nail and I noticed it was bleeding now.

There was silence for a few minutes and just as I had done previously, I watched as her eyeballs moved rapidly behind her closed eyelids as she relived the scene she was describing.

'Like I said, I was in the flat on my own by this time, although Dad hadn't died yet. I just sat in the corner for a long time. I was shitting myself and I thought I was going to die. There really was loads of blood!'

Abigail looked at me as though she thought I might doubt it.

'I am sure there was, Abigail. It must have been very frightening.'

'It bloody was! Then I had to think about what to do with them. You know, the babies.' She glanced at me.

'After I stopped bleeding and had cleaned up a bit, I put them in a doll's box. Actually it was the same doll's box that I had found in a skip with two broken dolls in it. You know the ones whose clothes I put on the babies?'

I nodded.

Abigail gave a long shuddering sigh.

'Like I said, I dressed them up in the doll's clothes. I thought about taking them outside somewhere to bury them, but I didn't have a garden and, anyway, I didn't know where I would get a spade to dig up the ground. I did say a little sort of poem or sort of a prayer for them and said goodbye to them. I told them that they were better off out of it, and they were.'

She gnawed at her nail again.

'Anyway, then I put the box on a blanket in the corner of the room and piled up loads of crap on top of them. The flat was always full of stuff so one more heap of it didn't make much difference. When their bodies were rotting it did smell a lot but then the house stank all the time anyway, so I guess it was just another smell to mingle in.'

She sucked her finger noisily, presumably to get rid of the blood she had drawn from biting her nail.

'Did you ever tell anyone about what happened?'

'Nope, I didn't say nothing till the pigs, I mean the police, asked me about it when they found the babies, after I was sent down.'

'Have you thought about what happened very much, over the years?' I asked.

Abigail looked thoughtful.

'I suppose so, now and again, mainly if I read something in the newspaper about babies or sometimes if I see babies out in the street in buggies. Although those babies didn't look anything like mine did, like

I said they looked a bit like aliens. I even had names for them.' She gave me a shy grin, as though she thought what she was saying was silly.

'Did you?' I asked. 'What names did you choose?'

'Dora and Laura. I always used to like *Dora the Explorer* when I was younger and then Laura rhymed with Dora, so I thought that was good, with them being twins and all.'

She glanced at me again to gauge my reaction. I smiled at her.

'Those are both very nice names,' I said.

* * *

Jessica Grisham of the University of New South Wales has found that the link between hoarding behaviour and traumatic events, such as losing a spouse or child, is especially important to consider in individuals exhibiting a late onset of hoarding symptoms, especially if those symptoms first appeared at the time of the event or shortly thereafter. Accumulating 'stuff' fills the emotional hole left by the trauma and allows individuals to avoid dealing with the pain. Later, removal of these items can trigger high levels of anxiety, especially if someone else gets rid of these items without the hoarder's permission.

When discussing their behaviour, many hoarders describe the 'rush' they experience when acquiring new items, especially if the item is free or on sale, and they will go to great lengths to justify purchases when questioned by friends or family members.

My challenge now was to find a way to help a young woman who had so many different problems. I felt sorry for Abigail because there was no doubt that she had suffered more than her share of bad breaks in life. But to stop her life continuing in the same destructive and harmful course, we needed to address the hoarding.

In Abigail's case I had tried psychodynamic psychotherapy and CBT with limited success. Where could I go now?

In fact, in the end, the answer came from one of the items that Abigail hoarded—one of the *Metro* newspapers that she managed to swipe from the local Tube station while the station attendant was looking the other way. In this particular copy, a girl who had been abused was celebrating the publishing of her book. Abigail haltingly read me the story in one of our sessions.

'She was only six when she first got abused! She got pregnant when she was eleven and then thirteen!' she said, her voice incredulous.

'Does it surprise you to read that story, Abigail?' I asked her.

'Too bloody right!' she said. Her eyes were bright with excitement. 'I never realised that other people, well, other girls, went through the same shit as I did! And she's only gone and written a bloody book!' She shook her head. 'D'you reckon that I could get in touch with her?'

'I don't know, Abigail, but it would be worth a try.' I was smiling to myself; this could be the breakthrough that I had been looking for. Abigail had clearly related to the story of this young girl whose experiences had so many parallels to her own.

I often reflect on how psychotherapy is not just a talking cure but also a telling cure. When clients can relate to a source of literature and at the same time are able to connect with their own narrative or story it can become an epiphanic moment. Literature has served since ancient times as a repository for collective human thinking and a source of what we would now call therapy.

I continued to see Abigail for the twelve months. The sessions had been funded through the court at the time of her trial. After she read the article about the girl who had a story similar to her own, Abigail did make further strides towards understanding and dealing with her hoarding, although this was slow. The council undertook to keep an eye on things so that they didn't get too far out of control and Abigail was transferred into the NHS to continue her therapy.

During the last consultation that I had with her, Abigail told me that she was still getting a lot of flashbacks, both to the night that her babies were born and also to the abuse she had suffered at the hands of her father and his friends. If ever I had wished there could be a quick fix for someone it would have been for Abigail, but the reality is that therapy is a marathon not a sprint, and can often be a tenuous tower of linked fragile pieces where only one needs to be disturbed to bring the whole lot crashing down.

* * *

Where hoarding is concerned, victims can often be the butt of humour; people's minds immediately go to the archetypal 'catwoman' who lives her life surrounded by clutter and cats, both dead and alive. But to understand the pain and the precursors that lead people to hoarding reveals that there is nothing at all amusing about this very debilitating condition.

Research into this previously largely overlooked condition is now giving hope that through psychotherapy we will have something to offer people who find themselves victims of hoarding.

SEVEN

Final thoughts

The majority of clients who come to see me for the first time will have had a stereotypical view of a therapist from a TV show or film in which a therapist always asked the person sitting across from them: 'How does that make you feel?'

When the question of how a client feels is well timed by a therapist it can lead to breakthroughs in identifying emotional patterns that are difficult to express and manage. There are, of course, countless ways to reconnect a client to their emotions in asking them how they feel.

For example, by asking, 'How do you feel about that?' (this will identify the topic of discussion and make sense for the client), or 'What sort of feeling is that?' (if the client is not sure what is going on and why they feel the way they do), or even 'What might somebody else be feeling at that moment?' or 'How does your partner/friend feel about what you have done?' (if I want to introduce another person's perspective).

Getting beyond our defences and into the parts of us that we don't understand, don't know and may not even want to acknowledge is complex and frightening. It takes trust and time to talk and express how we truly feel. And it is exactly this that I have tried to convey in all the case studies—how can I manage my emotions by understanding them and expressing them?

I have also demonstrated that the common denominator in all the case studies is the robustness of the therapeutic relationship. It is a very particular relationship in which the client seeking therapy learns about themselves through the prism of this relationship. As a client you talk about what has been going on, explore your responses and feelings and then you act on the insights you have learned, and then reach a point in therapy where you can ask yourself, 'Do I want to think, feel and react as I have reacted in the past or find a new way of being in this world?'

There is simply nothing that transforms your life as much as self-expression through the power of talking. This 'power of talking' creates a profound shift in consciousness when we share the truth.

Psychotherapy gives you the choice and allows you to try on these different ways of approaching your life. It does not rely on a magic wand or miraculous incantations that having been heard once will change you forever. Through my work as a therapist I have learned that all feelings, no matter how negative, can transform into love when you accept and express them.

Talking has immense power, and its impact depends entirely on how we wield it. Becoming more aware of the impact of talking, and the power it has on us and others, we can make more conscious, insightful choices about how we express ourselves and how we interpret others.

There are two dominant forces presented in all the case studies in this book: that of personal growth and that of personal fear. I have tried to show the reader that trying to create a world around us that is predictable and controllable will only lead to an avoidance of personal fear (a fear of 'change').

As humans we can view change as either exciting or frightening, but regardless of how we view it, we must all face the fact that change is always part of life.

As a therapist I understand change can be difficult for everyone. We can feel somewhat anxious at the prospect of a major upheaval or change in our lives. The problem comes when fear of change keeps us paralysed in situations that are not healthy or fulfilling.

You will have noticed in all the case studies I start by establishing a collaborative and empathic relationship with my clients. You will have noticed also that often I encounter resistance to change from those clients, which is typically evoked by personal experiences rather than a character flaw.

My approach is to allow my clients to be responsible for their own progress with the objective not to solve my clients' problems or even to develop a plan to solve them but rather to help each client to resolve his or her ambivalence, develop some momentum and believe that change is possible by eliminating the fear of resistance to change and allow healing to take place.

Our emotions need an outlet. They will always come out one way or another, because they are part of who we are. You may believe you have suppressed them, but what has happened is that your body and mind have stored them and, unless released, these emotions can manifest themselves physically and psychologically in chronic pain, anxiety, migraines, ulcers and other forms of illness. These physical manifestations are our body's way of telling us there are things that need to be healed.

Fortunately, you don't have to keep this fear inside you. Through the power of talking and self-expression you can let go immediately and allow your mind and heart to go back to the highest centre of consciousness it can achieve.

If you feel shame, let it go. If you feel fear, let it go. Eventually, you become wise enough to realise that you do not want that toxic stuff inside you.

I encourage you to begin now. Imagine what your life will be when you have begun this step-wise process towards wholeness. Learn to listen to your emotions. Strengthen your inner resources and embrace your determination to heal. Find out what's keeping you from living a life of independence by digging deep and discovering what's holding you back. You are deserving of every second of a joy-centred life free of the cumbersome burden of trauma and shame.

Acknowledgements

I wish to express my thanks to a number of people who gave me the support, advice and encouragement which enabled me to complete this book. I am grateful to my wife and three children. I owe a debt of gratitude to all of my mentors who have imparted your wisdom and compassion. In particular, Professor Alistair Ross, I thank you for your supervision and guidance, and for seeing me so clearly. I would also like to thank my friends and colleagues for being continual sources of inspiration and for standing with me as I take new steps personally and professionally. Thanks to everyone on the book at Phoenix Publishing House who helped me so much. Special thanks to Kate Pearce, the ever patient publisher, and Jane Compton, my amazing agent. Thanks are also extended to Andrea Henry, editorial director at Penguin Random House UK for her initial editorial support and encouragement. I am grateful to all my clients who, over the last three decades, honoured me with their brave vulnerability and authenticity. Thank you for sharing with me your vulnerable, hurt places. You inspire me with your courage to face your fears and confront your darkest spaces.

About the author

Stelios Kiosses is a psychotherapist and the Clinical Lead for Edison Education. He leads a multidisciplinary team responsible for ensuring the delivery and integration of evidence-based clinical and behavioural practices, as well as rigorous preparation and oversight for associate therapists and structured work experience for graduate psychologists. He studied psychodynamic counselling and clinical supervision at the University of Oxford and was previously trained in psychotherapy and experimental psychology at Sussex University. He is an associate member of the American Psychological Association and a member of both the British Association for Counselling and Psychotherapy and the British Psychological Society. He is a member of Corpus Christi College Oxford and a research collaborator with Professor Robin Murphy's Computational Psychopathology Research Group based at the University of Oxford.

Stelios currently teaches at Harvard University Extension School and has previously held teaching positions as a visiting senior research associate at Kings College London and as a visiting lecturer at Goldsmiths College University of London. He was originally appointed as an honorary senior lecturer in the Department of Psychiatry, University of

Birmingham, teaching on the MSc in Psychiatry (Family and Mental Health). In his public role he has acted as a UK TV psychologist and presenter for Channel 4's hit series *The Hoarder Next Door*, narrated by Oscar-winning actress Olivia Colman, and currently is patron of the Prince's Foundation School of Traditional Arts, one of HRH Prince of Wales' core charities.